ROMANS

BRINGING THE BIBLE TO LIFE

Genesis, by John H. Walton, Janet Nygren, and Karen H. Jobes
(12 sessions)

Esther, by Karen H. Jobes and Janet Nygren
(8 sessions)

John, by Gary M. Burge, Karen Lee-Thorp, and Karen H. Jobes
(12 sessions)

Romans, by Douglas J. Moo, Karen Lee-Thorp, and Karen H. Jobes
(12 sessions)

Ephesians, by Klyne Snodgrass, Karen Lee-Thorp, and Karen H. Jobes
(6 sessions)

Hebrews, by George H. Guthrie, Janet Nygren, and Karen H. Jobes
(8 sessions)

BRINGING
THE
BIBLE
TO LIFE

ROMANS

Celebrating the Good News

Douglas J. Moo
Karen Lee-Thorp

Series Editor, Karen H. Jobes

ZONDERVAN.com/
AUTHORTRACKER
follow your favorite authors

Bringing the Bible to Life: Romans
Copyright © 2008 by Douglas J. Moo, Karen Lee-Thorp, and Karen H. Jobes

ISBN 978-0-310-27652-4

Interior design by Michelle Espinoza

Printed in the United States of America

08 09 10 11 12 13 14 • 23 22 21 20 19 18 17 16 15 14 13 12 11 10 9 8 7 6 5 4 3 2 1

CONTENTS

SERIES PREFACE

Have you ever been in a small-group Bible study where the leader read a passage from the Bible and then invited group members to share what the passage meant to them? God wants to speak to each person individually through the Bible, but such an approach to group study can often be a frustrating and shallow experience for both leader and participants. And while the same passage can speak to people in various ways, the meat of the Word is found in what the biblical writer intended to say about God and our relationship to him. The Bringing the Bible to Life series is for those who are ready to move from a surface reading of the Bible into a deeper understanding of God's Word.

But the Bible, though perhaps familiar, was written in ancient languages and in times quite different from our own, so most readers need a bit more help getting to a deeper understanding of its message. A study that begins and ends with what a passage "means to me" leaves the meaning of the passage unanchored and adrift in the thoughts — and perhaps the misunderstanding — of the reader. But who has time to delve into the history, language, cultures, and theology of the Bible? That's the work of biblical scholars who spend their lives researching, teaching, and writing about the ancient Scriptures. The need is to get the fruit of all that research into the hands of those in small-group Bible studies.

Zondervan's NIV Application Commentary (NIVAC) series was written to bring the best of evangelical biblical scholarship to those who want to know *both* the historical meaning of the biblical text *and* its contemporary significance. This companion series, Bringing the Bible to Life, is intended to bring that material into small-group studies in an easy-to-use format. Pastors, Christian education teachers, and small-group leaders whether in church, campus, or home settings will find these guides to be an enriching resource.

Each guide in the series provides an introduction to the biblical book that concisely summarizes the background information needed to better understand the original historical context. Six to twelve sessions per guide, with each session consisting of eleven or twelve discussion questions, allow a focused study that moves beyond superficial Bible reading. Relevant excerpts from the corresponding NIVAC commentary provide easy access into additional material for those interested in going even deeper. A closing section in each session assists the group in responding to God's Word together or individually. Guidance for leading each session is included, making the task of small-group leadership more manageable for busy lives.

If you want to move from the biblical text to contemporary life on solid ground, this series has been written for you.

Karen H. Jobes, PhD
Gerald F. Hawthorne Professor of
New Testament Greek and Exegesis
Wheaton College and Graduate School

OF SPECIAL NOTE

Your experience with and understanding of the book of Romans can be deepened and enriched by referring to the volume on which it is based: *The NIV Application Commentary: Romans* by Douglas J. Moo, published by Zondervan in 2000.

Introduction

Andrea's best friend Julie doesn't care if there's a God. Andrea worries what will happen to Julie after Julie dies, but she's not sure she wants to believe in a God who wouldn't accept Julie into heaven.

Allen and Dave are business partners who disagree about whether or not a particular hobby is okay for Christians. The disagreement is putting stress on their work relationship.

Marcy is discouraged most of the time because it seems she can never live up to God's expectations. Stephen has a bad habit he feels guilty about but can't shake. Candace has an autistic son, and now she's been diagnosed with breast cancer. She struggles with where God is in the midst of such suffering.

All these people have questions whose answers are rooted in who God is, what the deepest nature and needs of humans are, and what God is doing about those needs. The apostle Paul wrote a letter to believers in Rome nearly two thousand years ago, and that letter has helped Christians in every generation sort out questions, emotions, and debates like these. The book of the Bible we call Romans lays out many of the foundational ideas of Christian faith.

PAUL

Paul was as smart, passionate, and dogged a missionary for Jesus Christ as he had once been as an opponent of the faith. Deeply Jewish, he had devoted his life to taking the news of the Jewish Messiah to non-Jews (Gentiles) throughout the Roman empire. He had logged thousands of miles on foot and by sea, spreading his message in what is now Turkey, Greece, and the

Balkans. After some twenty-five years planting Christian communities in key cities of the empire's eastern half, Paul desired to travel to the empire's far western edge to teach the gospel in Spain. He knew he'd need a base of operations in the west, and Rome—the glorious capital he'd never seen—was the obvious choice.

Paul knew a few believers in Rome, enough to spread a letter of introduction to the perhaps dozens of groups who met in homes around the city. Because his ministry was somewhat controversial, especially among Jewish Christians, he wanted the Roman believers to hear firsthand what he taught and why. He probably wrote his letter in AD 57, give or take a year, from the Greek city of Corinth.

Before embarking for Rome, we learn elsewhere, Paul first planned to travel to Jerusalem to deliver to Jewish believers some money he'd collected from his Gentile converts. Jewish-Gentile relations in the Christian community were sometimes tense, and Paul hoped this gesture would secure a bond of affection. Jewish-Gentile relations were much on his mind when he dictated Romans to his friend and scribe, Tertius, and that theme runs through the letter. But most of all, Romans details the faith Paul had hammered out "on the anvil of pastoral problems and debates"[1] over a quarter century of ministry.

THE ROMANS

Jews present in Jerusalem when the Holy Spirit was poured out at Pentecost (Acts 2:10) were probably the first to take the news of Christ to Rome. There were many synagogues in Rome, and the validity of Jesus as Messiah was probably debated there even before Paul's conversion. Along with Jews, Gentiles known as "God-fearers" probably attended those synagogues—these were men and women attracted to Judaism but not yet willing to undergo circumcision and embrace the Jewish law. The earliest house churches in Rome probably included both Jews and God-fearing Gentiles who learned of Christ in the synagogues.

"In A.D. 49 Emperor Claudius, out of exasperation with squabbles among the Jews about *Chrestus* (probably a reference to Jesus' claims to be the 'Christ'), issued an edict that required all Jews [including Jewish Christians] to leave Rome.... Overnight, therefore, the church in Rome became virtually 100 percent Gentile."[2] Jews were allowed to return a few years later, but Jewish Christians returned to communities dominated by Gentiles.

There were probably considerable tensions in the Roman church by the time Paul wrote, as those who shared Jesus' Jewish heritage now found themselves in the minority and no longer the leaders. It's no wonder, then, that Paul addressed Jewish law and Gentile arrogance so much in his letter. He wanted Jews and Gentiles to unite around a common vision of the gospel. He hoped to strengthen that gospel in them, and he hoped they'd help him take it to Spain.

"What is the 'good news' of Jesus Christ? Why do people need to hear it? How can they experience it? What will it mean for their future? And what does the good news have to do with everyday life? These large and basic questions form Paul's agenda in Romans."[3] These basic questions are still highly relevant and practical for us today.

NOTES

1. Douglas J. Moo, *The NIV Application Commentary: Romans* (Grand Rapids, Mich.: Zondervan, 2000), 17.
2. Moo, 18.
3. Moo, 23.

THE GOSPEL OF RIGHTEOUSNESS BY FAITH

Romans 1:1 – 32; 3:21 – 26

"Gospel" and "righteousness" are good church words. Their meaning is supposed to be obvious to any Christian who has been around awhile. But like the believers in Rome, we might have a general idea of what these words mean to teachers we've heard, but we might be hard-pressed to explain why this "gospel" about God's "righteousness" is a big enough deal to send a smart guy like Paul trekking back and forth across two continents. As Paul introduces himself to his Roman readers, he lays out this gospel of righteousness from God as the theme he wants to ignite in their imaginations.

WHAT IS THE GOSPEL?[1]

Read Romans 1:1 – 17.

1. How does Paul define the gospel in each of the following paragraphs? What is the good news he is called to announce?

Romans 1:1–6

Obedience that come by faith

Romans 1:16–17

Righteous by faith

THE RIGHTEOUSNESS OF GOD[2]

Read Romans 3:21–26.

Paul says the gospel is about "righteousness" (1:17; 3:21, 22). That's a word we'll see a lot in Romans, along with words that in Greek are related to it: "justify" and "just" (3:24, 26). These words have many Old Testament echoes. God's righteousness is, among other things, his saving activity. He upholds what is "right" by rescuing his people from trouble.

Paul says this rescue is for "all who believe." That is, it's not just for Jews, and it requires people's "faith" (1:5; 3:22, 26). It involves God's work in individual lives, personally and relationally. Righteousness is "the act by which God puts people who believe in right relationship to himself."[3]

2. For more than a century, our culture has defined the fundamental human problem as horizontal: estrangement in human relationships. We are alienated from each other (and from ourselves). But Paul says the fundamental human problem is vertical: estrangement from the only true God. As his letter goes on, he'll explain why he rates our vertical problem ahead of our horizontal one.

If our main problem is walls between us and other people, what kind of spirituality do we need?

listen

If our main problem is a chasm between us and a just God, what kind of spirituality do we need?

repentance

"Redemption" and "justify" are words from the legal world: " 'Justification' is what a judge does when he declares innocent the defendant in a trial."[4] "Redemption" comes from the world of the slave market: "One redeems slaves by purchasing their freedom."[5] We should avoid pressing this metaphor too far (such as by saying that Christ paid Satan, our previous owner), but we should understand that redeeming a slave is much more personal, powerful, and costly than redeeming a coupon.

3. Why can't God simply forgive our sins without Christ's sacrifice? Why would that violate the justice that is part of who God is?

EXAMPLE

4. Paul says "faith" is the response we have to make in order for Christ's sacrifice to affect our relationship with God. What is this "faith"? Is it, for example, intellectual assent to a set of facts?

EXAMPLE

GOING DEEPER

Christians who struggle to think of themselves as "worthy" to be in relationship with God need especially to understand this truth. We, in ourselves, are never worthy, not the best one of us. The gospel is precisely "good news" ... because it announces that God accepts us anyway; all that we have to do is receive his offer in faith—to be sure, a faith that must, by its very nature, always be accompanied by obedience (cf. 1:5).[6]

5. Why do you suppose it's so hard for many Christians to fully believe that God accepts them as they are, that all they have to do is receive God's offer by faith?

EXCHANGING THE TRUTH FOR A LIE[7]

Read Romans 1:18–32.

Having stated his theme—the good news that our relationship with God can be fixed—Paul goes on to explain why it needs fixing. He is well aware of the walls between people, but he wants to show that they are results of a deeper problem. That problem begins, he says, when people suppress some obvious truth (1:18).

6. Think about the truth Paul claims is obvious (1:19–20). How plain do you think that truth actually is in the world? What makes you say so?

If this truth isn't obvious to people, it's because their own choices have affected their capacity to think and discern (1:21). Three times he says "they exchanged" the truth of God for their own chosen god or sin. And three times he says God gives them over to the consequences of their choice.

7. In the first case, Paul says people exchange the worship of God for idols (1:22–23). In pagan Rome, people worshiped actual statues of various gods that represented fertility, the power of the Roman state, or divine guardians of their family. What are the idols in our culture today?

In the Roman world, sexual impurity (keeping mistresses, having affairs and homosexual liaisons) was not inconsistent with worshiping the gods of that culture (which sometimes involved visiting temple prostitutes). God simply gave people over to the consequences of their beliefs and actions.

8. Why would degrading one's body in sexual impurity (1:24) be a result of worshiping the wrong gods?

When Paul uses the words "natural" and "unnatural" in 1:26–27, he's talking about "the natural order of things *as ordained by God*."[8] Natural for him doesn't mean "biological" or "genetic" or "common in many cultures."

GOING DEEPER

Engaging in homosexual activity is to violate his [God's] created intention in making human beings male and female. Paul therefore endorses the Old Testament and Jewish view: Homosexual relations violate the order of creation established by God for all people. Believers ought to judge our culture by biblical standards and not force the Bible into the mold of our culture. Yet in a laudable insistence on maintaining biblical standards, we should not go further than Scripture. The Bible does not brand as sinful a homosexual orientation as such, only the indulgence of that orientation in lustful attitudes or actual sex.

Nor is it so clear that the Bible presents homosexual activity as a perversion worse than any other—as many Christians have thought.

To be sure, Romans 1 singles out homosexual activity for special attention. But Paul's purpose in doing so may not be because he regards it as a more serious sin than others but because he sees it as a particularly clear illustration of the violation of the created order. In any case, we are clearly called on to offer the same love and hope through the gospel to homosexuals that we offer to any caught up in any forms of sin.[9]

And lest his readers think sexual sin is the only or even the worst degradation, Paul also lists a catalog of nonsexual vices (1:28–32).

9. As you read 1:21–32, to what extent do you feel that Paul is talking about somebody other than you? To what extent is he talking about you? What makes you say that?

10. Does it seem reasonable to you that Paul talks about gossip in the same breath as murder (1:29)? Why or why not?

WHAT MAKES GOD ANGRY

All this discussion of specific sins is meant to explain something that we today need explained: Why is God angry? The instant Paul started talking about God's wrath in 1:18, many of us rolled our eyes. Isn't this idea of a wrathful God really just a way for authorities to keep us in line by scaring us? Or are these sins things that even a good parent or a just king would be angry about?

God's anger ... is never egotistic, as if he feels he needs to defend his dignity. Nor is it capricious, for God always acts justly, on the basis of his own unchangeable standards revealed in his Word to human beings....

Modern materialism, of course, denies the possibility of God's wrath. But perhaps a greater danger to the church is the persistent tendency in the midst of the awakened interest in "spirituality" to view God as a purely benign being. If God exists, so many people seem to reason, then he must be a good God who has our own interests at heart. Surely he could never be angry with us or do anything that might inconvenience us![10]

11. How do you respond to the idea of God's wrath (1:18)? For example, does it seem currently relevant or outdated? Is it hard for you to trust a God who expresses wrath? Is this a God you want to worship?

12. The bad news of 1:18 – 32 is meant to highlight the good news of 1:1 – 17 and 3:21 – 26. How would you summarize the gospel (good news) so far?

RESPONDING TO GOD'S WORD

IN YOUR GROUP:

Choose one or more objects that you think reflect God's eternal power and divine nature. You might choose a leaf, a pinecone, and a battery. Place them on a table in front of you. Spend some time giving thanks to God for what these objects reveal about him. Take turns offering a few sentences of thanks and praise. For example:

"Father, electricity is your invention. You created metals — nickel, cadmium — and gave them their properties when you formed the earth before we humans existed."

Close by having someone read aloud these words from Habakkuk 3:2 —

LORD, I have heard of your fame;
    I stand in awe of your deeds, LORD.
Renew them in our day,
    in our time make them known;
    in wrath remember mercy.

ON YOUR OWN:

Pray about God's righteousness — the right relationship with himself that he has given you if you have faith in Christ. If you have trouble living from a secure confidence that God loves you as you are, the first sentence of Romans 3:22 would be a good one to read over and ponder. Pray to see yourself as God sees you — not worthy (worthiness is irrelevant), but righteous.

NOTES

1. This section is based on *The NIV Application Commentary: Romans* (hereafter referred to as *NIVAC: Romans*), by Douglas L. Moo (Grand Rapids: Mich.: Zondervan, 2007), 35 – 57.
2. This section is based on *NIVAC: Romans*, 125 – 136.
3. Moo, 52.
4. Moo, 130.
5. Ibid.
6. Moo, 57.
7. This section is based on *NIVAC: Romans*, 58 – 70.
8. Moo, 66.
9. Moo, 67.
10. Moo, 65.

ADDICTED TO SIN

Romans 2:1–3:20

To treat a disease properly, we need the right diagnosis. Is this headache the result of a brain tumor or eye strain? Does the patient need surgery or new glasses?

Likewise, if we want to solve the pressing needs of humanity, we need to understand what's fundamentally wrong with humans. Philosophers have debated this matter for centuries. Is our basic problem ignorance? If so, then we need better education. Is our real problem an attachment to this world? If so, then Buddhism says we should meditate until we receive the enlightenment that this world and its sufferings are illusions. Does unequal distribution of wealth lie at the root of human suffering, as Karl Marx said? If so, then governments should have whatever power they need to redistribute wealth.

Paul says none of these diagnoses gets at the core human problem. He says: "People, by nature, are addicted to sin. They are imprisoned under it, unable to free themselves by anything they can do. Knowing this, then, God has sent to us not a teacher or a politician but a liberator—one who has the power to set us free from our sins."[1]

THE JEWS AND GOD'S JUDGMENT[2]

Read Romans 2:1 – 11.

In Romans 1:18 – 32, Paul depicted non-Jews as enslaved to sin. Not just good people who commit sins, but people whose minds and bodies are ensnared by sin. Now in chapter 2, he turns his attention to his fellow Jews. He speaks to a hypothetical kinsman directly as "you." Is it only Gentiles who are addicted to sin and need someone to save them from God's well-deserved wrath, or do Jews need that same Savior?

1. In 2:1 – 3, Paul challenges Jews for "passing judgment" on Gentiles for the acts described in 1:18 – 32. What kind of passing judgment does Paul oppose? How is it different from what Paul himself just got done saying about those acts?

2. Many Jews in Paul's day believed that because God had chosen them to be his beloved people, "his kindness, forbearance and patience" (2:4) would always lead him to forgive them. Therefore, they didn't need to worry about God's wrath against sin. According to Paul, why was that belief mistaken?

3. Setting aside Christ for the moment, Paul says that God in his justice has set up the world like this: In the end, everybody will get what he or she deserves (2:6). Those who persistently do good will win eternal life, while those who do wrong will be condemned. But who are these people who

Paul says will be given eternal life because of their good lives? Do you think they are:

a. Faithful Jews and moral Gentiles who lived before Christ came?
b. People now who don't know Christ explicitly but whose works are good enough to win God's approval?
c. People now who don't know Christ explicitly but who, by God's grace, are enabled to be saved and do works that God approves?
d. Christians who do good by grace?
e. Nobody? That is, theoretically someone who persisted in doing good could be saved by works, but in practice nobody does.

Which of the above (a through e) do you think is the best interpretation of 2:5 – 11? Who, if anybody, lives a good enough life to win God's approval? What leads you to that conclusion?

4. What can we learn about God from 2:1 – 11? (For example, what are his standards? How does he deal with people? Is he fair or unfair, reasonable or impossibly demanding?)

For Paul, being God's chosen people is a double-edged sword. God's Word is addressed first and foremost to the Jews. "When they respond positively, they are the first to receive blessing. But in the same way, they will also be the first to be judged for failure to respond."[3] Their status as the covenant people doesn't guarantee their immunity from consequences.

NATURAL LAW[4]

Read Romans 2:12–16.

We use the word "law" to refer to things as varied as man-made rules about how fast you can drive on the highway to normal tendencies of the material world, like the "law" of gravity. Almost every time that Paul uses the word, he's talking about the Torah, the law God gave through Moses. In Romans, Paul uses the word more generally to mean a rule or principle in 2:14, 3:28, 7:23, and 8:2. But otherwise he means the commandments given to Moses at Mount Sinai.

In 2:14 he says Gentiles are a "law" for themselves when "by nature" they do what the law of Moses commands. Here he affirms the Greek idea that there is a natural law—a set of universal moral norms—innate in all humans. This natural law is the foundation for all good laws of the state. It's the reason why one can talk about universal human rights, for example.

5. What evidence do you see in the world around you that there is a natural law built into all humans, regardless of culture? Or, what evidence do you see to the contrary?

6. Does anybody live so well by natural law that they can have a clean conscience when they stand before God someday? What does Paul say? What do you say, and why?

NOT EVEN LAW AND CIRCUMCISION ARE ENOUGH[5]

Read Romans 2:17–29.

God has given the Jews many privileges that the Gentiles don't enjoy, such as knowledge of God's will as recorded in Scripture and a calling to be guides for the blind and light for those in darkness (compare 2:19 to Isa. 42:6–7). These blessings are real. But *knowing* the Scriptures doesn't satisfy God. Only *obeying* them does. And while most Jews might be guilty of only "ordinary" sins (and many are model citizens, as Paul well knows), at least some went so far as to steal, commit adultery, or rob temples (2:22). "We have some evidence that Jews at this time were relaxing the Old Testament strictures against using precious metals melted down from idols"[6] — idols stolen from pagan temples. Paul isn't saying that most Jews committed such extreme acts, but he does think it's fair to say that, as a whole, his fellow Jews didn't live up to their high calling to be lights for the Gentiles.

7. Paul believes their special relationship with God has lulled his fellow Jews into a false sense of security. Are people who call themselves Christians also vulnerable to a false sense of security? How, or why not?

8. Why do you think some people see anti-Semitism in Romans 2, even though Paul himself is Jewish? What in Paul's words gives that impression?

9. How do you think Christians ought to relate to Jews? For instance, is it ever appropriate to share the gospel of Christ with a Jewish person? If not, why not? If so, how can we do this without being anti-Semitic?

GOD'S FAITHFULNESS[8]

Read Romans 3:1–8.

Many Jews of Paul's day believed God's faithfulness meant he would always do good things for his people. But Paul looked at the Old Testament and saw that God is faithful to his promises both when he blesses obedience and when he punishes disobedience.

10. God's righteousness is "his commitment always to act in accordance with his own character,"[9] a character that includes love, mercy, and holiness. His faithfulness is his commitment to keep his promises. In what ways is that good news for Jews? For Christians?

ALL UNDER SIN[10]

Read Romans 3:9–20.

Having exposed the sin of both Jews and non-Jews, Paul states his conclusion: "Jews and Gentiles alike are all under the power of sin.... Therefore no one will be declared righteous in God's sight by observing the law" (vv. 9, 20).

11. According to Paul, "People do not just commit sin, but they are 'under sin' ... helpless prisoners of sin ... addicted to sin."[11] Reflect back on what you've read in Romans 1–3. Do you think Paul is right? Does this sound like the non-Christians in your world? What makes you say that?

12. If Paul is right, what are the implications? For instance, how should this affect the way we view and interact with people whose lives seem as good as ours? How should it affect the way we interact with people whose lives are a mess? Should we avoid sin addicts, lest they contaminate our lives or influence our children? Why or why not?

RESPONDING TO GOD'S WORD

IN YOUR GROUP:

Pray for the Jewish people in your city, your country, and around the world. Ask God to reveal himself fully to them. Ask him to mature your love for people of other religions than your own, especially Judaism. Ask him to help you see others the way he sees them. Praise him for his righteousness (what does that mean?) and his faithfulness (what promises can you count on?).

ON YOUR OWN:

Reflect on the idea of addiction or slavery to sin. Do any people in your life come to mind? Is God putting his finger on any patterns in your own life? Pray for the sin addicts whom you know. How can you love them?

NOTES

1. Moo, 122.
2. This section is based on *NIVAC: Romans*, 71–83.
3. Moo, 75.
4. This section is based on *NIVAC: Romans*, 84–89.
5. This section is based on *NIVAC: Romans*, 90–101.
6. Moo, 94.
7. Moo, 101.
8. This section is based on *NIVAC: Romans*, 102–109.
9. Moo, 107.
10. This section is based on *NIVAC: Romans*, 110–124.
11. Moo, 111, 122.

THE RIGHTEOUSNESS OF GOD

Romans 3:21–4:25

Have you ever been inside a meat-packing plant? The stink is enough to make you a vegan. Slaughtered animals, blood up to the elbow—most of us are happy we don't have to deal with that. We like buying our meat wrapped in plastic on a Styrofoam tray.

Even less imaginable for us is God's temple in ancient Jerusalem, or the hundreds of pagan temples in Rome, where animals were slaughtered daily with elaborate rituals, their blood poured out in reeking pools. Animal sacrifice is now illegal in most Western countries.

So when Paul talks about Jesus as a human sacrifice, we often hold the idea at arm's length. Mel Gibson's film *The Passion of the Christ* flows with blood, and it's hard for us to take in the emotional impact and not ask, "Why? Why would God want this?" In explaining why, Paul takes us into God's astonishing heart.

JUSTIFICATION[1]

Read Romans 3:21–26.

God's plan to save us from our addiction to sin unfolds in stages. Salvation has a history—past, present, and future—and the coming of Jesus marks a new stage in that plan. "But now," says Paul (3:21), God is doing something new—still connected to what he was doing in the Old Testament, but also a big change.

1. Recall that righteousness is "the process by which God acts to put people in right relationship with himself."[2] How is the new way we are to be put right with God still connected to what God did in Old Testament times?

How is the new way we are made right with God a departure from the Old Testament?

The holiest part of the temple in Jerusalem contained the ark of the covenant, a gilded wooden box that held the tablets on which God's law was written. The ark's lid, or cover, was made of gold, with a golden cherub (angelic being) on each end. This cover was treated as the throne of the invisible God, who allowed his glorious presence to dwell in the temple. The Old Testament calls it the "atonement cover" (TNIV) or "mercy seat" (New American Standard Bible). The Greek translation of the Old Testament calls it the *hilasterion.*

In Romans 3:25, the TNIV renders *hilasterion* as "sacrifice of atonement." With this word, Paul refers to the annual sacrifice on the Day of Atonement (Lev. 16), when animals were killed and their blood was sprinkled on the atonement cover. This rite paid for the people's sin and turned away God's wrath against that sin. Paul sees this yearly atonement ceremony as a temporary measure — it didn't fully satisfy God's justice but looked forward to Christ, the adequate and final sacrifice.

2. What does the need for a sacrifice of atonement say about God and his justice? Why couldn't he simply forgive us without this sacrifice?

What does God's decision to make his own Son the sacrifice of atonement say about God?

GOING DEEPER

"Grace" ([Greek,] *charis*) is a key theological idea in Paul. He uses the word to stress that all God does on our behalf is done freely and without compulsion. It is God's very nature to be free from any outside "requirements" about how he acts. Nothing we can do requires him to put us right with himself. We receive what he does as a pure gift.[3]

3. In what way is Jesus' sacrifice an act of grace?

4. Why do you think our faith in Christ's blood (3:25) is a necessary response to that act of grace?

5. Why should falling short of God's glory (3:23) matter to us? Why isn't it enough for us to be simply human and imperfect?

6. From what you've studied so far in Romans, who were you (or who would you be) apart from Christ?

Who are you because of Christ?

7. Why is it valuable to reflect on this change?

BY FAITH ALONE[6]

Read Romans 3:27–4:25.

Paul has already said that faith is a necessary response to God's grace. He now elaborates on that point. Faith—not obedience to the Jewish law—is the response God requires in this new era. Between the times of Moses and Christ, obeying the law of Moses was a necessary response to God's generosity, but things are different now. This is so important to Paul that he spends all of chapter 4 citing Abraham, the revered ancestor of God's people, as an example.

8. Observant Jews (and, by extension, obedient people in general) are tempted to take pride in their obedience. Why is such boasting foolishness?

How is it spiritually harmful?

GOING DEEPER

Some Christians seem to equate "faith" with [only] agreeing to a set of doctrinal statements. Others think that allowing themselves to be baptized and participating regularly in communion is faith. Still others view faith as an emotion that they can stir up as a way of getting what they want from God.... Paul says three things about faith in 4:13–22 that go a long way toward filling out for us its meaning.

[First:] Faith is distinct from the law (4:13–14).... The law is something that must be "done," commandments that are to be obeyed. Faith, by contrast, is an attitude, a willingness to receive. Calvin likens faith to "open hands." ... In our achievement-oriented world, giving faith its necessary central place in our lives is not always easy to do.[7]

9. In what ways (if any) are you tempted to seek your validation, your sense of being okay with God and the world, from achievement rather than faith in Christ? What achievements have the strongest pull for you?

GOING DEEPER

[Second:] Faith has power not in itself but because of the one in whom we place our faith.... [T]he Bible does not talk about belief in miracles; it talks about belief in the God who works miracles.[8]

Abraham didn't just believe in miracles, in the possibility that his post-menopausal wife could become pregnant (4:17–21). He believed that God would keep his promise that she would conceive.

10. What are some promises that God asks you to believe?

[Third:] Faith is based on God's Word, not on the evidence of our senses.... The key to a full-bodied Christian experience is the ability to keep believing, day in and day out, that the ultimate reality is not what we see around us but what we cannot see—the spiritual realm.[9]

11. How is the faith God asks from you different from an emotion that you have to stir up in order to get what you want?

12. In summary, what can we learn from 3:21–4:25 about God's righteousness—what it is and how it works?

RESPONDING TO GOD'S WORD

IN YOUR GROUP:

Give group members a chance to share areas of their lives in which they are struggling to trust God. What one step of faith is God asking from each of you? Pray for each other about these issues. Close with worship along these lines:

> *Lord, thank you for making us right with you through Jesus' death. Thank you that none of our achievements or failures makes you love us any more or less. You are absolutely free and under no obligation to us, and yet you are generous to us beyond words. Thank you for forgiving us for all the ways we have fallen short of your glory. We open our hands to receive grace from you. We trust your promise to save us from the consequences of our sin, to give us life beyond death, to strengthen us in the trials of this life, and to transform us into the likeness of your Son.*

ON YOUR OWN:

Contemplate Jesus' sacrifice for you. What would help you put this event vividly into your mind? If words make a strong impression for you, slowly read one of the accounts of the crucifixion at the end of the four gospels. Try to put yourself into the scene, imagining the sights, sounds, and even smells. If you respond to pictures better than words, you might find a classic piece of artwork depicting the crucifixion and spend ten minutes praying over what you see. Your library may have a book of paintings. Collections of paintings are also available on the Internet (search for "Italian painting + crucifixion," for example).

NOTES

1. This section is based on *NIVAC: Romans*, 125–136.
2. Moo, 126.
3. Moo, 128.
4. Moo, 127.
5. Moo, 135.
6. This section is based on *NIVAC: Romans*, 137–167.
7. Moo, 162–163.
8. Moo, 163.
9. Moo, 164.

PEACE
AND HOPE

Romans 5:1–21

Peace. Hope. Joy. Who doesn't want those? All that and more comes to those who accept the righteousness God offers through Christ. "Sign me up!" we say.

But wait. Is that just hype? If peace means freedom from stress, few honest modern Christians can claim to have it. If our hopes are pinned on happy families, successful careers, and minimal suffering in this life, then many of us will be cruelly disappointed. So let's look at the fine print again. What exactly are the benefits of justification through faith in Christ? Why are we doing this? That's what Paul tries to help us understand—and get excited about—in Romans 5.

PEACE WITH GOD[1]

Read Romans 5:1–11.

1. Make a list of all the benefits of faith in Christ that Paul mentions in 5:1 – 11.

For many of us, the word "peace" calls to mind "an inner sense of security and serenity."[2] But in 5:1, Paul is talking about peace *with* God, "the objective position we find ourselves in because God has ceased to be hostile toward us and has reconciled us to himself."[3] The knowledge that God forgives us and welcomes us home should give us that inner security, but serenity is an illusion for anyone who hasn't been reconciled to God through Christ. It may be hard to believe that a friend who has acquired remarkable serenity through, say, Zen meditation is actually in more trouble than a Christian who battles anxiety, but that's what Paul says. He wants us to find inner peace by reflecting on what Christ has done for us.

2. Peace with God matters because it means we're saved from facing God's wrath on the day of judgment (5:9). On a day-to-day basis, how important is it to you that you'll be safe on judgment day? Why is that?

What are some here-and-now benefits of peace with God?

Faith in Christ also gives us access to stand in grace (5:2). "We not only get into relationship with God by grace; we live out that relationship day-by-day by grace."[4] Grace means that "all God does on our behalf is done freely and without compulsion."[5]

3. Give an example of how you live by grace in a typical situation.

4. Faith in Christ also leads to hope. Hope is longing for something (something you don't yet have) with the confidence that one day you'll get it. What do you think it means to hope for "the glory of God" (5:2)?

What do you passionately long for that you don't yet have? How high on your list of longings is God's glory? What, if anything, ranks ahead of it, and how does that affect the way you live your life?

Many of us long to hurt and struggle less. However, "Suffering is a normal part of a consistent Christian life."[6] Paul himself faced constant suffering. For a believer in Christ, suffering should lead not to despair, but to hope and even joy (5:3–5). "Just as resistance to a muscle strengthens it, so challenges to our hope can strengthen it."[7]

5. Some people who suffer grow in perseverance, a decreased attachment to things of this life, and a stronger hope in God's glory. Other sufferers lose faith in God's goodness and become bitter. Some get angry at God for a while but gradually grow stronger in faith and hope, while others sink into hopelessness. From what Paul says, what do you think accounts for these different outcomes?

6. How can we know that God loves us even while he's allowing something terrible to happen to us (5:5 – 8)?

THE REIGNS OF DEATH AND LIFE[8]

Read Romans 5:12 – 21.

Even when bad experiences urge us to doubt the benefits of life in Christ, Paul says we can be confident because our status as humans has changed. To understand his comparison between being "in Adam" and "in Christ," it's helpful to know how Jews of Paul's day looked at things.

For them, the bad parts of the human condition — distance from God, sins that cause so much human misery, and physical death that makes existence futile — all that could be summed up as life "in Adam." Jewish tradition held that while every person dies because of his or her own sin, Adam was in some way responsible for bringing sin and death to all people. We rugged individualists have trouble imagining how one man's long-ago sin could affect us. We insist that we alone determine who we are. "Modern psychology has revealed ways in which our apparently 'free' choices are, in fact, directed by our background and environment. But we still have difficulty with the idea that someone else's decision or act might decisively affect us."[9] Paul, however, takes for granted that we are interconnected, and that this ancestor's decision affects us all.

But if Adam set into motion the hopeless cycle of sin and death, Christ broke the cycle for all who by grace go from being "in Adam" to being "in Christ."

7. Paul repeats the word "gift" five times in 5:15–17. He also repeats the related word "grace" five times in 5:15–21. What is he trying to hammer home with all this repetition?

8. When he compares the situation "in Christ" to the situation "in Adam," he also repeats words about abundance: "how much more" (5:15, 17), "over-flow" (5:15), "God's abundant provision of grace" (5:17). What's his point here?

9. He contrasts the reign of death *over* Adam's descendants (5:17) to the reign of grace (5:21) and even our destiny to "reign in life through … Jesus Christ" (5:17). What images come to mind when you think about the reign of death over humanity?

What images come to mind when you think of yourself reigning in life?

Original sin refers to "the relationship between the first or original sin of Adam and the sin and death of all other people."[10] Christians debate just how Adam's sin affects us,[11] but we agree that sin and death are universal human problems, set in motion from the beginning.

GOING DEEPER Original sin may not make sense to many people; they may find it irrational or even unjust. But what better explanation for the extent and persistence of 'crimes against humanity'? When will we come to realize that genocide in Africa or in Yugoslavia is not abnormal but, in reality, just another manifestation of the kind of hatred that has marked human beings throughout the centuries?[12]

10. The Christian worldview attributes hatred, war, crime, economic inequalities, and other injustices to the fact that humans are "inherently bent away from God."[13] Think of a current social or political issue. How would this belief about human sinfulness affect the way you think about and respond to that issue?

11. Paul says Christ's sacrifice was for all people (5:18), but only "those who receive" this offer of grace will ultimately reign in life (5:17). That means some people are heading for wrath and hell. How do you respond to that idea? For instance, does it make you angry to think that God might let some of the basically decent people you know face hell? Does this belief seem outmoded and narrow minded? Are you indifferent to others' destiny as long as you and your loved ones are safe?

12. What in Romans 5 do you find especially encouraging?

What questions are you left with?

RESPONDING TO GOD'S WORD

IN YOUR GROUP:

Paul isn't asking sufferers to pretend to be joyful while in anguish, to read Romans 5:3 – 5 and snap out of it. In fact, later in Romans he tells us, "Rejoice with those who rejoice; mourn with those who mourn" (12:15). By listening to, mourning with, and encouraging those in pain, we enable them to experience God's love poured into their hearts. Your group can make a difference in whether someone suffers alone and struggles with hopelessness, or feels loved and perseveres toward hope. Allow some time for anyone in your group who is hurting to talk about it and receive prayer. Don't give advice; instead, "mourn with those who mourn."

ON YOUR OWN:

Reflect on the benefits of being justified by faith in Christ: peace with God; access into daily grace; God's love poured into your heart; hope; joy. Which of these do you experience and live? Thank God for them. Which of these seem more theoretical? Ask God to grip you with their reality. If contrary thoughts plague you — *God is mad at me. God is disappointed with me. God isn't there for me in my daily life. My situation is hopeless.* — decide whether you need to explore those voices to understand where they come from, or set them aside as distractions while you focus on what is true.

NOTES

1. This section is based on *NIVAC: Romans*, 168 – 178.
2. Moo, 174.
3. Id.
4. Moo, 175.
5. Moo, 128.
6. Moo, 177.
7. Moo, 171.
8. This section is based on *NIVAC: Romans*, 179 – 193.
9. Moo, 188.
10. Moo, 189.
11. See Moo, 189 – 190.
12. Moo, 192.
13. Id.

FREEDOM FROM SIN

Romans 6:1–23

What if you knew that no matter how badly you drove, you would never get a ticket, or be arrested, or have your insurance rates raised? What if you knew that your bad driving highlighted the police chief's graciousness toward you? Would you drive recklessly, even endangering other drivers?

That situation is similar to the one Paul addresses in Romans 6. What if you're absolutely safe from the penalty for sin? What if your sins highlight God's graciousness in forgiving you? Will you then sin recklessly because nobody's keeping score?

No real believer will do that, says Paul. Instead, a real believer will be thrilled to learn he or she is free not only from the *penalty* for sin, but also from the *power* of sin.

DEAD TO SIN[1]

Read Romans 6:1 – 14.

Christians live under a new regime. As children of Adam, we used to live under a regime in which we were ruled by sin and death. Now we live under a regime "in Christ" in which we're ruled by grace and life. Paul describes our move from one regime to another in terms of baptism.

GOING DEEPER

The New Testament presents water baptism as one component of a larger experience, which [James] Dunn calls "conversion-initiation." Faith, repentance, water baptism, and the gift of the Holy Spirit are the four key elements of this 'coming to Christ' experience.... [W]hen Paul refers to baptism in Romans 6:3–4, he intends to include faith, repentance, and the gift of the Spirit.[2]

1. According to 6:1–4, how does baptism (accompanied by faith, repentance, and the Spirit) affect us?

2. How important do you think baptism should be in a Christian community? Why?

GOING DEEPER

Our "old self" is Paul's way of describing our sinful condition as children of Adam. What is crucified, then, is that relationship [to Adam]. Our tie to Adam is dissolved; he and the sin and death he represents no longer dictate terms to us. Moreover, if the "old self" is Adam as corporate head of the human race, then the "new self" is Christ, corporate head of the church.[3]

3. Why is it hard for many Christians to believe that sin can no longer dictate terms to them?

4. Why is it inconceivable to Paul that a true Christian would think sin doesn't matter?

We are bodily creatures, and our bodies function largely by ingrained habit. A soldier who spends two years in a war zone develops the bodily habits of hypervigilance and instant reaction to danger. When he goes home to a land at peace, it can take a lifetime to retrain his body to believe he really lives in this new place. Especially in moments of stress, he can forget. Just as this veteran has to keep reminding himself that he's home, we need to remind ourselves that we live in the new regime of Christ. And just as the veteran has to retrain his body's reactions, so we need to retrain our bodies as 6:12–13 describes.

5. In what ways, if at all, is this analogy of the veteran soldier helpful to you? How is your situation like the veteran's?

6. What is involved in counting yourself dead to sin but alive to God in Christ (6:11)? How do you actually do this on a typical day?

7. Give an example of offering the parts of your body to God as instruments of righteousness.

WHAT GOD DOES AND WHAT WE DO[4]

Read Romans 6:15–23.

Most people want freedom and autonomy — the ability to do as they please. Paul argues that this is impossible. Our choice isn't between slavery and freedom. It's a choice between slavery to sin or to obedience.

8. Why isn't a non-Christian truly free? What enslaves him?

How does Paul's account compare with what you observe in people around you?

9. When we think of offering the parts of our bodies in slavery to sin, sexual sins naturally come to mind. What are some other bodily sins? For example, what are some sins of the mouth? Of the hands? How is consumerism a bodily sin?

Paul states things that are true, such as, "We ... died to sin" (6:2). He intersperses those statements with commands about what we should do to win the war against sin (6:12, 13, 19). We see here a balance between what God does and what he expects us to do. The commands are based on the truths. "God takes the initiative. In grace, he acts to help his people, and he asks them to respond."[5]

We mustn't separate our response from God's grace, as if we obeyed through our own unaided effort. We are justified by grace and we grow in obedience by grace.

GOING DEEPER

[W]e must root all of our obedience in those disciplines of the Christian life that put us in touch with God's own power: reading Scripture, worship, prayer.... We must always evaluate our own personal as well as the church's programs of Christian living against this test: Are they effective channels of God's grace?[6]

10. What channels of God's grace do you take advantage of on a daily basis? In a given week?

Are those channels of grace giving you enough help to obey God? How could you be more effectively open to grace?

11. Why isn't it enough to just "let go and let God" without any effort on our part?

12. How does a gossip stop being a gossip? What does God do? What does the person need to do? How might she avail herself of grace? What would it take, at a practical level, for her to offer her tongue in slavery to righteousness, leading to holiness?

Why does she need to remind herself about the new regime she lives under?

RESPONDING TO GOD'S WORD

IN YOUR GROUP:

Thank God for liberating you from slavery to sin. Offer him the parts of your bodies in service. You could begin by taking turns reading lines of this prayer, then add ideas of your own:

Lord, I give you these feet of mine that wander so easily. Teach them to dance to your tune, and to step on toes only when necessary.

My stomach, full of worries and hungers—let it growl for the food you give.

My hands that are always busy gripping, grasping, clenching, pulling, clinging. I give you them to dig with, hold hurt ones, mend broken things, touch in blessing.

I give you my shoulders to carry burdens of your choosing, not the weight of the whole world.

Open my eyes to see beauty, my ears to hear truth, and my mouth to speak goodness.

What is mine to do today?

ON YOUR OWN:

Lie flat on your back on the floor, or sit if lying on the floor is uncomfortable. Close your eyes and imagine offering each part of your body to God in turn. Start with your feet: what would it mean to offer your feet to God as instruments of righteousness? Where would and wouldn't you walk? As you move up your body, notice whether you carry tension in any of your muscles. Have you been offering those muscles to anger or anxiety? What would offering them to God involve? When you're finished (jaw, mouth, ears, eyes, brain), stand up slowly. Did anything come to you that you want to make particular note of?

NOTES

1. This section is based on *NIVAC: Romans*, 194–208.
2. Moo, 204.
3. Moo, 207.
4. This section is based on *NIVAC: Romans*, 209–216.
5. Moo, 214.
6. Moo, 215–216.

FREEDOM FROM THE LAW

Romans 7:1–25

Most people have a moral code they try to live up to. Maybe your parents taught you how good people do things. Maybe you know people who got a strong sense of how to live from the ethnic group they grew up in. For Paul, Judaism is the finest example of that, a test case of what would happen if God did remarkable things for an ethnic group and gave them a really good moral code to live by. He gave them a law that reflected his own goodness and holiness. But it failed to make them holy and good. All it did was highlight how stubbornly they did unholy things.

Paul deeply identifies with the Old Testament story of his people's failure. Their story is his story. Their story, in fact, is the story of anybody who grows up with or buys into a good moral heritage and then fails to live up to it. In Romans 7, Paul looks at Israel's experience with the law of Moses to show us why Christ changed the rules.

THE OLD WAY AND THE NEW[1]

Read Romans 7:1–6.

When Paul says that Christians have "died to the law" (7:4), he means that "[t]he believer has been set free from the commanding authority of the Mosaic law—period. What this means in practice is that no part of the Old Testament law stands any longer as a direct and unmediated guide to Christian living. Like a person who is free from the laws of the state of Indiana because she has moved to Illinois, so Christians are free from the law of the old covenant because we now belong to the new covenant."[2]

1. Just as we died to sin along with Christ, so we also died to the Old Testament law through Christ's death (7:4). Why do you think this was important for the Jewish and Gentile Christians in Rome to be clear about?

2. Paul says we "died to the law ... in order that we might bear fruit for God" (7:4). How is this different from dying to the law in order that we might do whatever we feel like?

GOING DEEPER

After proclaiming throughout Galatians that Christians are no longer under the Mosaic law, Paul warns them not to draw the wrong conclusions. God still expects believers to follow the command of love (Gal. 5:13–15) and to fulfill "the law of Christ" (Gal. 6:2).

Just what this "law of Christ" might be is not clear from Paul's teaching. Some interpreters think it consists only in the example of Christ. Others think it is simply the command that we love our neighbors as ourselves. But the many commandments in Paul's own letters, along with the plural "commands" in 1 Corinthians 7:19, suggest a broader interpretation: the example of Jesus and the commands he and his apostles issue as a guide to the Spirit-filled life.[3]

3. How is serving "in the new way of the Spirit" different from serving "in the old way" of the law of Moses (7:6)?

4. We think serving "in the new way of the Spirit" includes obeying New Testament commands. Do you agree, or does that sound like more legalism? Explain your thinking.

WHY THE GOOD LAW BROUGHT DEATH, NOT LIFE[4]

Read Romans 7:7–12.

The "I" in this passage isn't Paul as an individual. He was never "alive apart from the law" (7:9), because he was born as an heir of Adam and as a Jew under the law. The "I" is Paul speaking in solidarity with his people, Israel. He's "alive to the corporate dimension of life."[5] Israel's story is his story.

5. What does Paul say about himself ("I") in 7:7–12 that is true of Israel but not technically true of him as an isolated individual?

What does he say there that you think is also true of him as an individual?

6. How easy is it for you to think of yourself as part of a people across continents and centuries, whose story is your story? Why is that?

Why is or isn't this an awareness that you think Christians need?

The story of Israel is that the law arouses "sinful passions ... in [their] bodies" (7:5 NIV). It keeps them "from coming to know Christ (v. 4) or experiencing the new life of the Spirit (v. 6)."[6] It even stimulates rebellious people to sin more, because telling them not to do something just makes them want to do it more (v. 8). But the law isn't to blame. Blame sin, which uses the good law to bring death.

7. In what ways do the moral codes of other groups fail similarly?

LIFE UNDER THE LAW[7]

Read Romans 7:13 – 25.

Paul continues to speak of "I" in this passage. Some readers think he's talking about his personal experience as a mature Christian. Others think he's talking about what it's like to be an immature Christian. There are strong arguments to be made in support of both of these interpretations, but along with most Pauline scholars, we take a third view. We think Paul is describing his life as a Jew under the law: delighting in the law of Moses, desperately trying to live up to it, but too enslaved to sin to do what he knows he should. No matter which of these views is correct, "The central claim of this text is undebatable: The law cannot free us from spiritual death."[8]

8. Why, according to 7:13–25, can the law not free us from spiritual death?

One reason why people strongly debate whether Paul is here describing his experience as a mature Christian is that they want to make sense of their own experience. If they find themselves struggling with sin so intensely that they often feel defeated and wretched, it's a comfort to think that Paul struggled too. If they don't struggle that intensely, it's easier to say that isn't the normal Christian life. "Each of us brings a certain view of what the Christian life 'must be like' to this text."[9]

9. To what extent do you identify with the struggle Paul describes in this passage? How does that affect the way you interpret it?

10. If Paul is talking here about the struggle of a dedicated Jew and not that of a mature Christian, what, if anything, does that say about the place of intense struggle against sin in a "normal" Christian life?

If this isn't the way the Christian life is supposed to go, why do so many Christians see themselves in these words?

11. What do Christians who struggle intensely need from other Christians?

GOING DEEPER

Romans 7 is about the "religious person." Paul is looking at the very best of human beings outside of Christ. We can then think of people in our day who fit this profile, people who have a deep and sincere desire to do good and find approval with their god. Indeed, in the pluralistic environment of our day, people completely dedicated to various religions and beliefs are all around us. But the experience of Paul and other Jews under the law proves the point: Sincerity is not enough. As long as people are "sold as slaves to sin," sincerity by itself can never lead to genuine fulfillment of God's law.[10]

12. If it's not enough for people to "have a deep and sincere desire to do good and find approval with their god," how can Christians best be friends with such people?

RESPONDING TO GOD'S WORD

IN YOUR GROUP:

Hand out small blank pieces of paper and pens. Take five minutes of silence to think about one of these statements:

- "For I have the desire to do what is good, but I cannot carry it out" (7:18).
- "The evil I do not want to do—this I keep on doing" (7:19).

Think of how one of these was true in your life before you trusted Christ, or how it's true now. Write down a few words about the good you desired to do but didn't, or the evil you did. Or the sin you struggle with now, or the good you find yourself currently unable to do.

Pass around a basket and let each person tear up his piece of paper and drop the bits into the basket. Take some time to thank God for:

- Freeing you from slavery to this sin, or
- Freeing you from the hopelessness of living up to your moral code, or
- Offering you, even now, the grace to take another step away from slavery in this area.

ON YOUR OWN:

There are many benefits of growing up with a strong moral code. But one of the hard legacies of such an upbringing is sorting out the differences between what our parents or community taught us to do and what Jesus and the New Testament writers teach us to do. Is "work hard and get ahead" in the Bible? What about "clean up your room"? Make a list of "commandments" you learned growing up. Ask God to show you which of these he wants you to live by and which ones you can let go of. If you feel you grew up with little guidance about how to live, chances are you learned by example, or by reaction against what you saw. What rules to live by did you come up with?

NOTES

1. This section is based on *NIVAC: Romans*, 217–224.
2. Moo, 223–224.
3. Moo, 222–223.
4. This section is based on *NIVAC: Romans*, 225–232.
5. Moo, 230.
6. Moo, 225.
7. This section is based on *NIVAC: Romans*, 233–246.
8. Moo, 234.
9. Moo, 243.
10. Moo, 244.

LIFE IN
THE SPIRIT

Romans 8:1–39

Who are you? How do you define your identity? Many of us identify ourselves according to the roles we play: spouse of so-and-so, parent of these children, job or career description, volunteer work, and so on. Others find identity in belonging to an ethnic group, or in a form of entertainment or hobby (video gamer, fan of this musician, science-fiction lover, gardener). In a mass society where few people know us intimately, we may proclaim our identity to strangers by a style of dress, a T-shirt logo, or a personalized license plate.

Paul understands how essential identity is. He wants us to find the core of who we are in being "in Christ" as opposed to "in Adam" or "slaves of sin," or "under the Jewish law." He wants "in Christ" to be the identity that shapes how our minds think, what our wills choose, and what action we take with our bodies.

FLESH VERSUS SPIRIT[1]

Read Romans 8:1–13.

Paul says we can look at the old and new regimes "in Adam" versus "in Christ" from another angle as "in the flesh" versus "in the Spirit." The TNIV renders "flesh" (Greek: *sarx*) in various ways to get at what the word signifies to Paul: "sinful nature" (8:3, 4, 5, 6, 8, 9, 12, 13) or "sinful humanity" (8:3). Paul is talking about "a condition, natural to people, in which God and the spiritual realm are left out of account. To be 'in the flesh' (7:5; 8:8–9) is to be helplessly trapped in this situation. Thus, people naturally think in a 'narrowly human' way ('the mind of the flesh' — 8:5–6) and live in a 'narrowly human' way ('live [or walk] according to the flesh' — 8:4–5). In contrast, Christians, who no longer are in this condition, must not act as if they were. They must cease living 'according to the flesh' (8:13)."[2]

1. Paul says every real Christian is in, or controlled by, the (Holy) Spirit, not in the flesh/sinful nature. How does he make that clear in 8:1–13?

2. Living in the flesh is our former identity. Living in the Spirit is who we are now. Yet in 8:12–13, Paul says we have to keep choosing to live according to our new identity. If we have a new identity, why do we have to keep putting to death the habits of the old one? Why doesn't it happen automatically?

3. What's the allure of life in the flesh/sinful nature?

The words "mind" (v. 6) and "have their minds set on" (v. 5) include intellectual activity ("thinking" in the narrow sense), but go beyond it to involve the will also. [A mind-set] is our fundamental orientation, the convictions and heart attitude that steers the course of our life.

As such, having the "mind-set" of the Spirit is the crucial "middle" step between existence in the sphere of the Spirit (v. 9) and living according to the Spirit (v. 4b). Cultivating a Spirit-led, Spirit-filled disposition of heart and mind is necessary if we are to live in a way that pleases God.[3]

4. How are you forming your mind-set? What (television shows, reading matter, music, conversation, etc.) do you feed your mind that reflects the value system of the flesh? What do you feed your mind that reflects the ways of the Spirit?

5. If being in the Spirit is fundamentally who we are as Christians, why aren't we more often drawn to creatively and passionately engage our minds with God in prayer and Scripture?

SUFFERING AND GLORY[4]

Read Romans 8:14–30.

To be in the Spirit is also to be God's adopted child, sharing now in his firstborn Son's suffering but destined to be heirs of his glory. In our feel-good culture, we're inclined to think suffering is a sign that God has abandoned us or that he doesn't exist. Paul wants us to see suffering as normal and to respond to it with hope.

6. Suffering and hope was one of the topics of session 4. What additional reasons for hope does 8:14–30 offer?

GOING DEEPER

We groan *because* we have the Spirit. Once the Spirit, with his demand for holiness, enters our lives, we sense as never before just what God wants us to be. As a result, the Spirit increases our frustration at not meeting God's standard and our yearning to be what he wants us to be.[5]

7. Sometimes we (along with God's whole nonhuman creation) hope the way a woman in labor hopes: with plenty of groaning, sweating, and desperate longing for the pain to end (8:22–23). How can that kind of groaning be consistent with faith and patience?

GOING DEEPER Most of us have probably heard someone (perhaps ourselves!) applying Romans 8:28 something like this: "Yes, you may have lost your job, but you can be sure of getting an even better one; because 'all things are working for good.'" ... The difficulty with this application is that it interprets "good" from a narrow and often materialistic perspective. From God's perspective, "good" must be defined in spiritual terms. The ultimate good is God's glory, and he is glorified when his children live as Christ did (v. 29) and attain the glory he has destined them for (v. 30; cf. vv. 31–39).... The "good" God may have in mind may involve the next life entirely.[6]

8. A tragedy (a child's death, for example) isn't good in itself. Nor does God kill children for the spiritual benefit of parents. What, then, does Paul want to say in 8:28 (and in this passage more broadly) to those of us who suffer tragedies?

"Glory" (8:17, 18; cf. 8:21, 30) isn't a cotton-candy word. Think of something with weight and light, with the brilliance and gravitational pull of a million suns. Looking at God's glory, even angels shade their eyes. Some heavy, bright reflection of that glory will someday be revealed in you.

9. When imagining your future glory, what thoughts or feelings come to mind?

Why should looking ahead to glory affect how you live now?

MORE THAN CONQUERORS[7]

Read Romans 8:31–39.

For three chapters, Paul has been urging us to get focused on our identity and security in Christ. Now he wraps up this theme with a trumpet flourish intended to stir both feeling and action.

10. What emotions is Paul trying to stir up in us in this passage?

11. What is he trying to persuade us to do?

12. To be in Christ is to be securely loved. How real is that for you? How has (or hasn't) the conviction that you are securely loved affected your emotions, thought patterns, or actions?

To be in Christ is also to be secure against nagging guilt or fear of condemnation. To what extent is that a settled issue inside you, or to what extent do you struggle with guilt? How has or hasn't studying Romans helped you so far?

RESPONDING TO GOD'S WORD

IN YOUR GROUP:

Consider playing a song that talks about God's love for us in Christ, or the freedom from condemnation he gives. Group members can listen in silence or sing along, and then follow the song with their own words of thanks and praise. If you can't play music, you could have someone read aloud some lyrics, such as these by Samuel Crossman:[8]

My song is love unknown,
My Savior's love to me;
Love to the loveless shown,
That they might lovely be.
O who am I, that for my sake
My Lord should take, frail flesh and die?

ON YOUR OWN:

Jesus has a man's body and face, but God the Father doesn't. Nevertheless, imagine for a moment that he does. Close your eyes and picture God looking at you. What expression is on his face? Ask him to show you how he looks at you. Does he look disappointed that you're still stuck in the same old habits? Does he look irritated or downright angry? Hurt? Does he look at you with the indulgent smile of one who knows you're a rascal but is too nice a guy to confront you? Can you imagine a strong, fearless face seeing you with intense, burning love? Can you imagine him wild with joy at the glory he's finally revealing in you? Prayerfully reflect on the word "beloved" or the word "glory." Ask God to show you how he sees you as beloved or glorious.

NOTES

1. This section is based on *NIVAC: Romans*, 247–259.
2. Moo, 254.
3. Moo, 257.
4. This section is based on *NIVAC: Romans*, 260–280.
5. Moo, 267.
6. Moo, 277–278.
7. This section is based on *NIVAC: Romans*, 281–289.
8. Samuel Crossman, "My Song Is Love Unknown," *The Young Man's Meditation* (1664, public domain). Cited April 27, 2007 online: *http://cyberhymnal.org*.

THE PROBLEM
OF ISRAEL

Romans 9:1–10:21

A aron is an observant Jew. He enjoys Sabbath worship and keeps the law of Moses to the best of his ability. He is gener-ous to charities and passionate about justice. He knows the names of family members who died in the Holocaust. In his eyes, con-verting to Christianity would be a betrayal of his family, both living and dead.

Richard is agnostic. His older sister is Christian, and she has more than once explained the gospel to him and tried to get him to read the Bible. But Richard isn't interested in whether or not there's a God or what will happen to him after he dies. He does good work as a scientist and tries to be a good person. His sister loves him and worries about what will happen to him.

Firoozeh lives in a tiny village in Iran, immersed from birth in the teachings and practices of Islam. She has never been exposed to the gospel, as her country doesn't grant visas to Christian missionaries.

If Paul were alive today, he would care deeply about Aaron, Richard, and Firoozeh. Paul is Jewish to the bone, and it kills him to think about what will happen to his fellow Jews who reject Christ for reasons he can easily understand. He knows what it's like to love a family member who isn't interested in Christ. And he aches for people like Firoozeh who have never had a chance to hear the gospel. In Romans 9 – 11, the puzzle at the front of his mind is about the Jews: what is the God of Abraham up to if Gentiles are flocking to the gospel while Jews are staying away in droves? Investigating this puzzle leads him to even deeper issues, such as whether God is reliable and whether he's fair.

IS GOD RELIABLE?[1]

Read Romans 9:1 – 13.

The Old Testament is about promises God made to Abraham and how those promises played out in the actions of God and Abraham's descendants. If the gospel isn't part of the master plan of those promises, then it can't be good news, because it would mean that God has thrown his promises out the window. And if God abandons promises whenever he feels like it, then we can't trust him.

Here's the problem: God called the Israelites, adopted them, and promised them glory. Now the Jewish Messiah has come, yet far more Gentiles than Jews have embraced him. Has God's calling failed? Have his promises failed? If so, we too should be skeptical when he offers us adoption and glory.

1. Why does Paul feel such anguish about Jews who don't believe in Christ (9:1 – 5)?

Do you feel that way about anybody? If so, who?

God's word hasn't failed (9:6). He's not unreliable, because not all of Abraham's biological descendants are his spiritual descendants. Abraham had two biological sons, Isaac and Ishmael, but only Isaac inherited the covenant. Likewise, Isaac's wife Rebekah had twins; God chose Jacob but not Esau. (Romans 9:7 – 13 makes far more sense if you're familiar with Genesis 12 – 33. In fact, Romans 9 – 11 relies so heavily on the Old Testament that it illustrates how important it is for Christians to read the Old Testament.)

2. The quotation in 9:13 means "I chose Jacob, not Esau." What does it say about God that before these brothers "had done anything good or bad" (9:11), God had already chosen one to inherit his promises but not the other?

Some interpreters think Paul is saying that God chooses individuals like Isaac and Jacob based on the faith he foresees they will have. Others think Romans 9 isn't about individual salvation, that Isaac and Jacob represent the nation of Israel that God chose. But we think Paul's vocabulary ("children of the promise," "election") and the context suggest that Paul is talking about God choosing individuals, not nations, and that he's saying God "chooses based on his decision to choose,"[2] not based on the individual's faith.

3. What's attractive about seeing God as "all-powerful and completely free in his actions"[3], choosing people based simply on his freedom to choose? What, if anything, bothers you about seeing God this way?

Emotional responses aside, as you read the text of Romans 9:6–13 do you see Paul talking about God choosing individuals or nations? If individuals, then on what basis?

IS GOD JUST?[4]

Read Romans 9:14–30.

This idea that God chooses people before they do good or bad raises the question of whether God is fair. But what is fairness or justice? "Determining right or wrong, what is just or unjust, demands a standard for measurement. That standard is ultimately nothing less than God's own character.... God, therefore, acts justly when he acts in accordance with his own person and plan."[5]

Paul illustrates this point with the case of Egypt's Pharaoh. In recounting the plagues by which God freed the Israelites from slavery, Exodus 4–14 refers to the hardening of Pharaoh's heart twenty times. Sometimes the text says God hardened Pharaoh's heart, sometimes Pharaoh hardened his own heart, and sometimes the verb could be taken either way. Because Pharaoh refused to free the slaves, people all over that part of the world heard about what God did to help them.

4. According to Romans 9:15–23, how did God pursue his own purposes through Pharaoh?

5. Why does Paul think this was a perfectly just way for God to treat Pharaoh?

GOING DEEPER

God's decision to destine some people to wrath comes *after* (in a logical sense) that sin. God's "hardening," then, does not cause spiritual insensitivity; it maintains people in the state of sin that they have already chosen. When God chooses people to be saved, he acts out of pure grace, granting a blessing to people who in no way deserve it. But when he destines people to wrath, he sentences them to the fate they have already chosen for themselves.[6]

Many people feel it's unfair for God to rescue some of us from our sin but leave others to their fate. Our culture teaches that all people should be treated equally and that we should be masters of our fate. We feel our eternal destiny should be up to us (by living rightly or having the right faith), not God. But if God gave us what we actually deserve, all of us would get the death sentence because we're all involved in Adam's sin (5:12 – 21).

6. Biblical scholars disagree on the correct interpretation of this difficult passage. Does this view of God sound to you like what Paul is teaching? Is it consistent with what you see elsewhere in the Bible? Explain your view.

How does Paul's portrait of God in Romans 9 affect you?

Does it make you want to praise God for his greatness and mysterious purposes, or pull away in mistrust? Why is that?

DOES HUMAN RESPONSE MATTER?[7]

Read Romans 9:30–10:21.

Now, after hearing so much about God choosing however he likes, we're back to a passage where "righteousness" and "faith" are key words.

GOING DEEPER

However much we may want to claim that salvation is based on God's choice, we must also insist that the human decision to believe is also both real and critical. We are not puppets in God's hands, passively moving as he directs. We are responsible human beings, called by God to exercise faith in his Son. The evidence of Scripture compels us to maintain a fine balance at this point.[8]

7. In 9:30–10:13, what reasons does Paul give for the fact that many Jews aren't receiving salvation?

   What role does human decision play?

8. This passage explains human destiny from a different angle than the previous passage did. If you put both passages together, what place does a person's faith (or lack thereof) have in his or her salvation?

What place does God's sovereign choice have? How do you relate human faith and divine choice in your mind?

GOING DEEPER

[When Paul says "Christ is the end of the law" (10:4), he means] "Christ is the culmination of the law." ... I [Moo] am interpreting the [Greek] word *telos* as a combination of the ideas of "end" and "goal." ... With the coming of Christ, the goal toward which the law was pointing has been reached.... Let's picture Israel as the runner, the law as the race, and Christ as the finish line. What Israel has failed to understand, Paul is saying, is that the finish line has been reached. The Messiah and the salvation he brings have come. Thus, the "race" has attained its end and goal — or, to use the best English equivalents, its "culmination" or "climax."

As a result of Christ's coming and bringing the law to its culmination, righteousness is now available for everyone who believes.[9]

9. If the purpose of the Old Testament law was to point toward and lead toward Christ, what value do you think the Old Testament has for us?

10. We began this study with the stories of three people: Aaron, Richard, and Firoozeh. In light of what Paul says in 9:30 – 10:21, what do you think Paul would like to say to Aaron? What would Paul's emotions be as he says this?

11. How do you think Paul would explain Richard's lack of interest in the gospel?

How would Paul feel about Richard and relate to him?

What might he say to Richard's sister?

12. In light of 10:14 – 15, what do you think Paul would say about Firoozeh, who has never had a chance to hear the gospel?

How important is it for Christians to try to reach Firoozeh with the message of Christ? And what if, despite our efforts, no missionary ever does reach her?

RESPONDING TO GOD'S WORD

IN YOUR GROUP:

We don't know how the free, sovereign God takes our prayers into account, but he does. Take a few minutes to write down three or four names of non-

Christians you would like to pray for. These could be family, friends, coworkers, a gym employee, a hair stylist, a parent of your child's friend. Then as a group offer these names to God in prayer, asking him to call them to himself. Pray also for people who live in countries where they aren't exposed to the gospel. Pray for missionaries whom you know.

ON YOUR OWN:

Read the following passage slowly several times, and reflect on who God is. What emotional responses do you have to this God? Can you imagine this God beholding you with love, calling you, commissioning you to serve him?

> *I am the LORD, and there is no other;*
> *apart from me there is no God....*
> *I form the light and create darkness,*
> *I bring prosperity and create disaster;*
> *I, the LORD, do all these things.*
> *You heavens above, rain down my righteousness;*
> *let the clouds shower it down.*
> *Let the earth open wide,*
> *let salvation spring up,*
> *let righteousness flourish with it;*
> *I, the LORD, have created it.*
>
> Isaiah 45:5, 7–8

NOTES

1. This section is based on *NIVAC: Romans*, 290–308.
2. Moo, 307.
3. Moo, 308.
4. This section is based on *NIVAC: Romans*, 309–324.
5. Moo, 310.
6. Moo, 317.
7. This section is based on *NIVAC: Romans*, 325–352.
8. Moo, 307.
9. Moo, 330–331.

ISRAEL'S FUTURE

Romans 11:1 – 36

The end of the world. It fascinates us. We buy books, watch movies, and listen to preachers forecasting it. The details vary, but what's significant is that we Christians, along with traditional Jews, expect an end. Neither Hinduism nor Buddhism produced speculation about the end of the world, because those religions envision history as an endlessly repeating cycle. The Jews changed the world by claiming that, according to God, history had a beginning and is heading toward an end.

Paul says little in Romans about the end of history, but what he does say affects how we view issues from personal salvation to Middle East politics. In chapter 11 he talks about the Jews' present situation before God and then sketches his hopes for them in the future, at the end of history. That future glimpse has sparked an amazing amount of speculation about what's ahead for all of us.

THE PRESENT: THE ELECT AND THE HARDENED[1]

Read Romans 11:1 – 10.

Before he looks into the future, Paul talks about the situation of Israel as it was in his day. God's promises to the patriarchs don't guarantee salvation to all of their physical descendants. Does that mean the Jews are now just one ethnic group among many to him? No, says Paul. As a group they still have a role to play in God's unfolding plan.

1. Paul speaks of "a remnant" (11:5) within Israel. He calls them "the elect" (11:7). How does what he says here about the remnant of Jews echo what he said in chapters 9 – 10 about the Jews of his generation?

   How does what he says about the many other Jews who are "hardened" (11:7) echo what he has said earlier?

Paul affirms God's faithfulness by saying that God irrevocably called the nation of Israel. But he explains the Jews' meager response to Christ by saying that God elects only some Jews for salvation. He's balancing two teachings from Jewish tradition: corporate election and individual election. And he insists that "God has not completely abandoned the nation in order to concentrate only on some within it."[2]

2. Many Christian groups have seen themselves as remnants of the elect holding onto the true faith amidst a much larger number of hardened people. What are the spiritual benefits of seeing oneself as part of a remnant?

What are the potential risks?

3. There are also churches in which some people believe they are saved because they were born into that group and participate in its rites: baptism, religious education or Sunday school, church attendance, and so on. How is this situation similar to the error Paul saw many Jews making?

THE PRESENT: THE OLIVE TREE AND THE GRAFTED BRANCHES[3]

Read Romans 11:11 – 24.

Paul says this situation, in which only a remnant of Jews respond to the gospel, is temporary. It furthers God's plan for salvation history.

4. How has the Jews' rejection of Christ served God's salvation plan?

Paul describes a sequence of Jews rejecting Christ → Gentiles receiving blessing → Jews coming to faith and receiving blessing. Some interpreters think he's describing "a continuing oscillation, which repeats itself many times over the course of history as Jews and Gentiles interact with one another." However, we agree with interpreters who see "a single, linear sequence, which leads from the Jewish rejection and Gentile acceptance of [Paul's] day to a climax of greater Jewish response to the gospel in the last days."[4]

5. Consider the word picture of the olive tree (11:17–24). Why have some Gentile believers been boasting about themselves and looking down on the Jews?

Why are they foolish to do so?

GOING DEEPER

There is only one olive tree, only one people of God. The roots of the tree are planted in Old Testament soil. They are the patriarchs.... The Old Testament people of God was drawn almost entirely from the nation of Israel—although with notable exceptions (e.g., Rahab, Ruth, Uriah). But now, at the turn of the ages, God extends his grace and invites Gentiles to join his people on an equal footing with Jews.... Faith in Christ, the bringer of salvation, is now necessary. Yet Paul's imagery makes clear that the turn of the ages did not bring into existence a new people of God. Rather, Gentiles join the already existing people of God, "true Israel."

From this perspective, then, we see how wrong is the common idea that the church has "replaced" Israel.[5]

Gentiles have been grafted into Israel, and we now call that Jewish-Gentile people of God "the church." Some Gentile believers assume "the church" is a Gentile institution that leaves Jewish believers on the sidelines. But Paul sees the church as rooted in Judaism, with Gentile believers welcome but by no means superior.

6. What are the implications of seeing the Christian community as rooted in Jewish soil? How does that affect the way we treat Jewish believers and unbelievers? How does it affect the way we practice our faith?

7. How do you understand the warning in 11:19–22, which suggests that believers could be "cut off" from the tree if they fail to continue in God's kindness?

How does that fit with God's promise to save us by grace, apart from anything we could do to earn salvation?

How does it fit with the assurance that nothing can separate us from God's love in Christ (8:31–39)?

THE FUTURE: ALL ISRAEL WILL BE SAVED[6]

Read Romans 11:25–32.

Gentiles have no reason to be conceited, because they are simply grafted into God's people, which used to consist mainly of ethnic Israelites. And one day, as history draws toward its goal, "all Israel will be saved" (11:26).

"All Israel" could mean the whole church (although in Romans 9–11 Paul has consistently used "Israel" to mean ethnic Israel). It could mean the elect Jews of every generation who have been faithful. However, we believe otherwise.

GOING DEEPER

In agreement with most commentators, we think "all Israel" refers to the totality of national Israel. This does not mean that every single Jew will be saved....

Paul here predicts the salvation of a significant number of Jews at the time of Christ's return in glory. The present "remnant" of Israel will be expanded to include a much larger number of Jews who will enter the eternal kingdom along with converted Gentiles.[7]

These Jews will be saved because of faith in Christ (as Paul entertains no other way for anybody to be saved).

8. Do you agree with this understanding of the statement, "All Israel will be saved"? Explain your reasons for your view.

9. How do you think this understanding should affect the way Christians relate to Jews?

GOING DEEPER

What Paul predicts in this chapter is a spiritual revivification of the Jewish people. He says nothing here, or anywhere else in his teaching, about the return of Israel to Palestine or about its political reconstitution. Any belief that God has promised Israel a political presence in the end times must come from other passages in Scripture.[8]

10. Do you think Paul's teaching about the Jews' future should affect our nation's foreign policy toward the political state of Israel? Toward the Palestinians? Toward other Middle Eastern countries? Explain your view.

GOING DEEPER

I [Moo] taught for some years with a colleague who was Arab in background. He could never understand why American evangelicals consistently took the side of Israel in every Middle East dispute. The Arab side was never considered; Israel, whatever it did, was always in the right. Even if we believe that God has promised to give Israel their land again and make them a nation, we have no right to accord Israel such blind allegiance. For one thing, we have no way of knowing if the present Israel is the Israel in which God will fulfill his promises. More important, God calls us to love all people and to treat all people with respect. We have no right to overlook injustice when it occurs, whether in Israel or anywhere else. Moreover, we certainly have no right to ignore the legitimate rights and aspirations of the Arab people.[9]

11. How do you respond to these thoughts about the state of Israel and the Arab people?

A RESPONSE: WORSHIP AND HUMILITY[10]

Read Romans 11:33–36.

Paul started chapter 9 with grief for his fellow Jews. He ends his reflection on their future with words of wonder and worship. As much as he wants his readers to understand the tension between their security in Christ and the risks of complacency (11:19–22), as much as he wants them to understand what lies ahead for Israel, he's all too aware that God's thoughts are "more intricate and marvelous than we could even imagine."[11]

12. As you look back at what you've learned about God's ways from his dealings with Israel (chs. 9–11), what stands out to you?

RESPONDING TO GOD'S WORD

IN YOUR GROUP:

Use Romans 11:33–36 as a springboard for worship.

Oh, the depth of the riches of the wisdom and knowledge of God!
How unsearchable his judgments,
 and his paths beyond tracing out!
"Who has known the mind of the Lord?
 Or who has been his counselor?"
"Who has ever given to God,
 that God should repay them?"
For from him and through him and to him are all things.
To him be the glory forever! Amen.

Read this passage aloud together, then add your own words of praise for God's wisdom, his choices, his plans and deeds. How have you experienced his wisdom? His mysteriousness? How does it affect you that he is the source, sustainer, and goal of everything?

ON YOUR OWN:

Write a prayer to God, telling him how you see him. Praise him for who he is, and also tell him what you don't understand about him. Write down things he's done for which you are grateful, such as choosing you to be part of his family. Notice the emotions you feel as you write: Gratitude? Joy? Wonder? Frustration? Numbness? Tell him why you feel those things.

NOTES

1. This section is based on *NIVAC: Romans*, 353–361.
2. Moo, 359.
3. This section is based on *NIVAC: Romans*, 362–375.
4. Moo, 363.
5. Moo, 371–372.
6. This section is based on *NIVAC: Romans*, 376–388.
7. Moo, 379.
8. Moo, 386.
9. Moo, 387.
10. This section is based on *NIVAC: Romans*, 389–392.
11. Moo, 392.

THE
TRANSFORMED
LIFE

Romans 12:1 – 21

You love your toddler. She's perfect just the way she is. Not that you're blind to her faults—the food hurled to the floor with a stubborn whine, the hysterics at bedtime, the love-hate relationship with pull-up diapers. You forgive all this drama because she's only two, but you're also committed to helping her grow out of it.

Having adopted you into his family, God enjoys you even more than you enjoy your little girl, just the way you are. Yet he's also committed to helping you grow up so you can fully live like who you are: an adult member of the family. He'll help you do what you couldn't do on your own, but you need to cooperate. In Romans 12, Paul talks about how to grow up as a member of God's family.

BODY AND MIND[1]

Read Romans 12:1 – 2.

Here in a few sentences we have "the essence of the believer's response to God's grace in the gospel of Jesus Christ. It functions as the heading for all the specifics Paul will unpack in the subsequent chapters."[2]

1. "Mercy" (12:1) is literally "mercies" plural. What mercies have you experienced?

What mercies has Paul described in Romans 1 – 11?

As he said in chapter 6, Paul again says that the response to grace is to offer our bodies.

GOING DEEPER

Worship is the way we live, not what we do on Sunday morning. . . . We worship God, says Paul, by giving ourselves in sacrificial service to our Lord. We are to serve him every day, every hour, every minute.

Paul deliberately uses the word "body" ([Greek,] *soma*) to describe what we are to offer to God. This word focuses on the "embodied" nature of our persons, reminding us that we are physical beings, interacting with a material world. . . . One of the greatest temptations in the Christian life is to bifurcate the "spiritual" world from the material, to begin thinking that only certain parts of our lives have eternal significance.[3]

2. Give some examples of how you can offer your body as a sacrifice to God in your daily life.

The word translated in 12:1 (NIV) as "spiritual" (Greek, *logikos*) probably means rational and informed by the realities of the gospel. Both Jews and pagans offered animal sacrifices and too often thought all that mattered was doing the ritual without regard to their attitude. The Jewish philosopher Philo argued that "that which is precious in the sight of God is not the number of victims immolated but the true purity of a rational spirit [*pneuma logikon*] in him who makes the sacrifice."[4] Similarly, Paul says, "Worship that pleases God is 'informed'; that is, it is offered by the Christian who understands who God is, what he has given us in the gospel, and what he demands from us."[5]

3.   Why does it matter that our worship be informed by who God is, what he has done, and what he asks of us?

Why isn't it enough to worship with emotional excitement?

Paul says we're transformed into people who worship all day long not by willpower or by emotional highs, but by the renewing of our minds. "When we change the way we think, we change the way we live."[6] The vast majority of our feelings and actions are automatic responses — someone cuts us off on the highway, and we respond automatically with rage and aggressive driving, or a shrug and a prayer. It all happens too fast for us to decide in the moment not to be aggressive. So to change how we respond on the road, we have to get at attitudes deeply ingrained in our minds that propel those automatic reactions.

4.   What are some deeply ingrained attitudes that might lie behind a person's aggressive and sometimes angry driving?

5. We talked in session 7 (questions 4 and 5) about changing what you feed your mind. What could a person feed his mind that would help the Holy Spirit transform the attitudes behind his aggressive driving?

GOING DEEPER

Many preachers, intent on getting their people to obey God, fall into a legal approach to Christian ethics.... As a result, Christians tend to lead a double life: "Christian" in that behavior for which they have been taught laws, but essentially secular in those areas of life not touched by those laws. A Christian may not abort her baby, because she has been taught not to do that. But she may harbor racist attitudes or cheat on her taxes without batting an eye. If renewing the mind is as important as Paul says, then the goal of ministry should be to form Christian minds in people.[7]

6. How can a church help to renew its members' minds so that they respond in Christian ways to things like driving, taxes, and ethnic differences?

HOW COMMUNITY HELPS[8]

Read Romans 12:3–8.

Christian community is an essential aid in renewing our minds and transforming our actions. It's so non-optional that Paul spends the rest of this chapter describing how we need to think about and function within community.

7. The first item on Paul's list of renewed ways of thinking is "Do not think of yourself more highly than you ought" (12:3). Why do you suppose this is an essential first step in changing our lives?

Why is it an essential attitude for healthy relationships with other Christians?

Paul urges us to value the church as God's body here on earth. "[W]hen Paul uses body terminology for the church, he is thinking of Christ's death on the cross as the means by which that community was brought into being."[9] Just as we used to be "in Adam," part of his body, so now we are "in Christ" — joined to him and to each other in such a real way that it's impossible for us to function as Christians without each other. And Paul would likely raise his eyebrows if we said we belonged to the universal church but didn't want to be involved with any local, face-to-face gathering of the church.

8. What reasons for involvement in a face-to-face local church does Paul give in 12:3 – 8?

GENUINE LOVE[10]

Read Romans 12:9 – 21.

Another essential attitude shift is from pretend love to sincere love.

The Greek for "sincere" is *anypokritos* (lit., not hypocritical). The underlying word was often applied to the actor who "played a part" on the stage. Christians can avoid love that is mere "play-acting" if they put into practice the commands that follow.[11]

9. Choose one of the instructions in 12:9–16, and explain why it is an essential element of non-hypocritical love within a Christian community.

Romans 12:17–21 takes love to an even costlier level. Don't retaliate against those who harm you. Show kindness to enemies "with the hope that they will become ashamed of their actions and seek the underlying reason why [you] can respond with such love."[12] To keep peace with even unbelievers, do what they will see as right — up to the point where their approval would come at the expense of what is right in God's eyes. Your own interests come second not only to God's but to other people's! This is how Christ lived.

10. We'll talk in session 11 about whether this nonviolence and non-retaliation applies even to the state. Think of it now in your own life. Give some examples of what this might look like for you. Is Paul asking for you to be a doormat who never says no?

11. Why do you think Paul wants us to live like this, when the potential costs are so high?

12. What are one or two aspects of the transformed life in Romans 12 that you believe you most need to develop in your own life?

RESPONDING TO GOD'S WORD

IN YOUR GROUP:

A few sessions ago you prayed to offer the parts of your body in service to God. Because we need to offer and re-offer our bodies to God daily, it would be worthwhile to revisit that subject, and offer your bodies to God again. Here is a centuries-old prayer that talks about offering both body and mind to God. Notice the body parts it mentions: eyes and mouth. Those might be good parts for some group members to focus on. Others might want to focus on the mind (notice that this poet sees the heart as the organ that thinks one's deepest thoughts). You can read the prayer aloud together, and then each of you can read aloud the line that he or she wants to focus on.

God be in my head, and in my understanding;
God be in mine eyes, and in my looking;
God be in my mouth, and in my speaking;
God be in my heart, and in my thinking;
God be at mine end, and at my departing.[13]

ON YOUR OWN:

Save a few minutes at the end of each day this week to ask yourself the question, "What did I feed my mind today?" Reflect back on what you saw on television, heard on the radio, saw on the Internet, read, listened to. Is your brain diet renewing your mind or conforming it to the world? Offer your brain diet to God.

NOTES

1. This section is based on *NIVAC: Romans*, 393–400.
2. Moo, 394.
3. Moo, 397–398.
4. Moo, 396.
5. Id.
6. Moo, 398.
7. Moo, 399.
8. This section is based on *NIVAC: Romans*, 401–407.
9. Moo, 406.
10. This section is based on *NIVAC: Romans*, 408–419.
11. Moo, 409.
12. Moo, 413.
13. *The Sarum Primer* (1558, public domain). Included in *The Hymnal: 1940. According to the Use of the Episcopal Church* (New York: The Church Hymnal Corporation, 1940), hymn 466.

LOVE
AND LAW

Romans 13:1–14

The framers of the U. S. Constitution mistrusted governments. They created three branches — the President and his cabinet, the Congress, and the courts — in order to keep any one branch from wielding too much power. That mistrust of government has deep roots in the American psyche, so when Paul talks in Romans 13 about submitting to the governing authorities, many American Christians flinch.

Paul and his readers in Rome lived under a government whose corruption and brutality remain legendary to this day. At the time Paul was writing, the burden of taxes and fees was so heavy that people were going beyond grumbling to resistance. There was a tax revolt in AD 58, just a year after Paul probably wrote this letter. Some Roman Christians might have felt that avoiding conformity with the world (Rom. 12:2) meant rejecting the authority of any of the world's institutions, especially the government. Paul had no illusions about the empire, but he took a different view.

THE CHRISTIAN AND THE STATE[1]

Read Romans 13:1–7.

1. What reasons for submitting to the government does Paul give in 13:1 – 7?

In calling for submission, Paul isn't necessarily demanding obedience to every government mandate. Submission isn't equivalent to obedience.

GOING DEEPER

To be sure, they overlap [and] submission is usually expressed through obedience [but] submission is broader and more basic than obedience. To submit is to recognize one's subordinate place in a hierarchy established by God. It is to acknowledge that certain institutions or people have been placed over us and have the right to our respect and deference. . . .

But implicit always in the idea of submission is the need to recognize that God is at the pinnacle of any hierarchy. . . . Paul assumes that one's ultimate submission must be to God and that no human being can ever stand as the ultimate authority for a believer.[2]

2. When might a Christian have to disobey the government because of submission to God? Give some examples.

3. What are some laws that Christians should obey in a spirit of submission, even though they might not want to?

LOVE, AGAIN[3]

Read Romans 13:8–10.

Speaking of what we owe our leaders (13:6–7) reminds Paul of what we owe everyone (13:8), and that brings him back to the subject of love. *Love* means different things to different people, so Paul takes pains to define what he means.

4. Some people define right and wrong by the standard of what seems loving to them. But Paul says genuine love seeks what is good for the other person (12:9, 21) and avoids harm for that person (13:10). Ultimately, God gets to define what is good. How could this standard of pursuing good and avoiding harm help someone who:

- Avoids confronting friends about sin because that doesn't feel loving?

- Blasts other people about their sins?

- Wants to have sex outside marriage because they and the other person "love" each other?

Love has fulfilled and therefore replaced the law of Moses (13:8, 10), but because to love is to seek the other person's good, no one who truly loves will murder, commit adultery, steal, or covet. And while the commands of the old covenant are no longer binding on Christians, we are expected to obey the commands of Jesus and the apostles. The foundational New Testament commands are to love God and others (Matt. 22:34–40). There are also other New Testament commands, such as "Do not lie to each other" (Col. 3:9) and "Flee from sexual immorality" (1 Cor. 6:18) that are both expressions of love and commands in their own right.

5. Suppose your friend asks you if another friend really said something nasty about him. By answering truthfully you may damage the relationship between the two of them. Would it be more loving to lie? Would lying be the right thing to do? Explain why you see it as you do.

Is there another alternative?

6. Is it legalistic to treat "Do not lie to each other" and "Flee from sexual immorality" as commands that Christ expects you to obey? Explain your view.

GOING DEEPER

Biblical love ... is not an emotion. It is an attitude, a mind-set.... We are commanded to love; it is therefore a choice we make, a matter of the will.

To be sure, I do not think any of us can love in the way the Bible asks us to without the enabling grace of God.... But our wills are involved. The Spirit may foster love within us. But it is our job to cooperate with the Spirit in developing a consistent mind-set of love toward others and to work actively at putting love into effect in the various relationships we find ourselves involved in.... [And] love must be defined in God's terms.[4]

7. How does a person cooperate with the Holy Spirit in developing a consistent mind-set of love toward others?

UNDERSTANDING THE TIMES[5]

Read Romans 13:11 – 14.

Love, submission to the state, and the whole Christian way of life make sense if we understand the times in which we live. "The day" Paul speaks of is the day of the Lord promised by the Old Testament prophets.

GOING DEEPER

[T]his present evil age is ending soon and the time of God's final victory is at hand. . . . Recognizing that dawn is upon us and that the Lord Jesus may return at any time to finalize his victory, we need to live even now as if that day has come.[6]

8. Why should expecting Christ's return motivate us to live ethically?

9. What if Christ doesn't return for another century or another millennium? Does that mean we're foolish to live ethically now? Explain your thoughts.

10. What are some of the "desires of the sinful nature" (literally "flesh," 13:14) that we shouldn't even think about gratifying?

Paul singles out some behaviors that are inappropriate for people of the light (13:13). Some Christians today have strong views about what is appropriate in the way of entertainment and what is commonly called "partying." Others, sometimes in reaction against a strict upbringing, prefer to emphasize our freedom in Christ and downplay concerns about "behaving decently." This is especially confusing territory for young adults: Is there a level of raunchiness or violence in entertainment that isn't good for us, even if it's not strictly forbidden? What about premarital sexual interactions?

11. How can 13:11 – 14 help us make decisions about entertainment, sexuality, and social discourse without falling into legalism?

12. In what one or two areas is God calling you to fuller submission, deeper love, or more wisdom in living appropriately?

RESPONDING TO GOD'S WORD

IN YOUR GROUP:

A good focus for worship would be the day of Christ's return. Play a favorite song from a CD, or have someone read aloud the words of this hymn by Frederick Lucian Hosmer[7]:

Thy kingdom come! on bended knee
The passing ages pray;
And faithful souls have yearned to see
On earth that kingdom's day.

But the slow watches of the night
Not less to God belong;
And for the everlasting right
The silent stars are strong.

And lo, already on the hills
The flags of dawn appear;
Gird up your loins, ye prophet souls,
Proclaim the day is near.

The day in whose clear-shining light
All wrong shall stand revealed,
When justice shall be throned in might
And every hurt be healed.

When knowledge, hand in hand with peace,
Shall walk the earth abroad;
The day of perfect righteousness,
The promised day of God.

ON YOUR OWN:

Feed your mind on songs, words, and pictures of the day of the Lord. Read aloud to yourself one or more of the songs of praise in Revelation 19:1 – 10. If you can, go outdoors for a walk just before dawn, and think about what it means to live at a time when dawn is just about to break.

NOTES

1. This section is based on *NIVAC: Romans*, 420–432.
2. Moo, 429.
3. This section is based on *NIVAC: Romans*, 433–438.
4. Moo, 416.
5. This section is based on *NIVAC: Romans*, 439–445.
6. Moo, 443.
7. Frederick Lucian Hosmer, "Thy Kingdom Come! On Bended Knee," (1891, public domain). Included in *The Hymnal: 1940. According to the Use of the Episcopal Church* (New York: The Church Hymnal Corporation, 1940), hymn 391.

LIFE TOGETHER

Romans 14:1–16:27

There's nothing like a good fight between Christians about things that really matter: Are drums appropriate for worship music? Which Bible version is best? If Jane's twelve-year-old daughter wants to wear high heels to church, but her friend Jill thinks that's wrong because the media over-sexualizes preteen girls, what should Jane do?

Issues like these have split churches and broken friendships. And it's all too common for churches in a town to compete for members by talking down the practices of other churches. Paul had heard that Christians in Rome had different views on some issues that in his mind weren't central to the gospel. Believers—for whom love fulfilled every law—were sniping about what foods real Christians should eat and what holidays they should keep. In response, he laid out some timeless principles for dealing with "disputable matters."

DON'T CONDEMN EACH OTHER![1]

Read Romans 14:1–12.

This dispute between the weak and the strong probably had to do with practices from the Jewish law. Even though the Jewish Christians in Rome agreed that keeping the law of Moses wasn't necessary for salvation, they'd kept it all their lives, and they couldn't bring themselves to abandon the kosher food laws and Sabbath customs. Meat from pagan butchers made them gag, so they'd rather be vegetarians. And treating Saturday like any other day just felt wrong. They cringed in disgust when they saw Gentile Christians stuffing themselves with pork—and Gentile Christians rolled their eyes right back at what looked to them like rigid traditionalism.

GOING DEEPER

Paul sides with the strong [probably mostly Gentile Christians] on the basic issues involved, but his main concern is to get each group to stop criticizing the other and to accept each other in a spirit of love and unity.[2]

1. What reasons for not judging and looking down on each other because of "disputable matters" (14:1) does Paul give in 14:1 – 12?

"Weak in faith" in this passage doesn't mean weak belief in Christ generally but overly sensitive in "one's convictions about what that faith allows him or her to do. The weak in faith are not necessarily lesser Christians than the strong."[3]

GOING DEEPER

The Scripture commands us to do certain things (e.g., to worship God), and it forbids us from doing certain other things (e.g., to commit adultery). But many other things are neither commanded nor prohibited—God's people have the freedom to do them or not to do them.[4]

2. Give some examples of things you think are "disputable matters" that Christians are free to do or not do.

3. Are there any things that Christians are free to do that you don't personally feel comfortable doing? If so, what are they?

How do you tend to view Christians who do things you're uncomfortable with?

How do you tend to view those who aren't comfortable doing things you feel free to do?

GOING DEEPER Nevertheless—and this is a vital point—we cannot extend the tolerance Paul demands here to *all* issues.... [H]e takes a different approach toward people who are violating a clear teaching of the gospel. Such people are not to be tolerated but corrected, and, if they do not repent, are to be cut off from the life of the church (see 1 Cor. 5). We must, then, be careful to apply the tolerance of Romans 14:1–15:13 to issues similar to the one Paul treats here.[5]

4. How can we know whether something is a belief or practice we should tolerate (and even welcome) or one we should not tolerate?

GOING DEEPER

Scripture is clear about some doctrinal matters. But the evidence on others is not so clear-cut. Thus, professing Christians take positions along a wide spectrum. Some are "minimalists," insisting on only a very few beliefs (or none at all) as essential to the faith.... At the other end of the spectrum are "maximalists," who insist that any Christian who wants to enter into fellowship must cross the "t" and dot the "i" on an interminable list of doctrinal, ethical, and social issues.[6]

DON'T CAUSE YOUR BROTHER OR SISTER TO STUMBLE![7]

Read Romans 14:13 – 15:6.

Even though Paul identifies with the strong who feel free to eat or drink anything, he warns them not to use their liberty in a way that harms a brother or sister. "[H]e is *not* saying that we must refrain from activity that another believer may disagree with."[8] In order to reach pagans with the gospel, Paul did plenty of things that more conservative Jewish Christians disapproved of. The stumbling (14:13, 20), falling (14:21), or being destroyed (14:15) that Paul worries about happens when, by doing something freely, we tempt a fellow believer to do what we're doing, even though he or she believes it's wrong. This peer pressure undermines their conscience. Our free behavior is also a stumbling block if it so offends someone that they abandon the faith because of it.

5. "But if anyone regards something as unclean, then for that person it is unclean" (14:14) because it doesn't come from faith (14:23). Why doesn't Paul just tell such a person to get over his too-sensitive conscience?

6. What are some things that Paul says in 14:13–23 are more important than our rights and freedoms?

7. Allen and Dave are partners in an engineering firm. Some fellow engineers in their town get together a couple of times a month to play poker. Dave joins them because he thinks it's a harmless way to connect with colleagues, have fun, and be a Christian presence among unbelievers. He doesn't think he or anybody else there is at risk of losing too much money or becoming a gambling addict. Allen doesn't feel comfortable with the poker nights: some of the men smoke, most of them drink alcohol, and Allen thinks gambling is something a Christian shouldn't do or support. It bothers him that Dave participates.

   How do you think Allen and Dave should approach a conversation about poker night? (If you're in a group, consider having two group members act out the conversation. Then let the whole group critique how it went according to the principles Paul lays out in Romans 14.)

8. After this conversation, Dave decides to go to poker night and Allen knows that. What thoughts and feelings should Allen have about Dave the next day?

What thoughts and feelings should Dave have about Allen the next day?

9. Paul cites Christ as the prime example of one who was more concerned with others' needs than with pleasing himself (15:1 – 3). From what you know about Christ, who did he try to please? Who didn't he try to please? Where did pleasing himself fit into his priorities?

How is this relevant to situations where Christians disagree?

10. When Christians disagree with what those in another church, another part of their denomination, or another Christian organization believe or do, what principles or ground rules do you think they should follow in dealing with that disagreement?

GREETINGS AND BLESSINGS[9]

Read Romans 15:7–16:27.

This final section of Paul's letter gives us a great deal of information about the earliest believers and about Paul. But we'll focus on a few portions that have lasting relevance to us: Paul's prayers and blessings for his readers.

11. What can we learn about God—his character and priorities—from 15:5–6, 13, 33 and 16:25–27?

12. As you look back at this study of Romans, what insights stand out to you? What does God most want you to know and act on?

RESPONDING TO GOD'S WORD

IN YOUR GROUP:

Ask four group members each to read aloud one of these prayers from the end of Romans. They can read the prayers as written or change "you" to "us" or "we," and "yourselves" to "ourselves."

> *"May the God who gives endurance and encouragement give you the same attitude of mind toward each other that Christ Jesus had, so that with one mind and one voice you may glorify the God and Father of our Lord Jesus Christ." (Rom. 15:5–6)*

"May the God of hope fill you with all joy and peace as you trust in him, so that you may overflow with hope by the power of the Holy Spirit." (Rom. 15:13)

"The God of peace be with you all. Amen." (Rom. 15:33)

"Now to him who is able to establish you in accordance with my gospel, the message I proclaim about Jesus Christ, in keeping with the revelation of the mystery hidden for long ages past, but now revealed and made known through the prophetic writings by the command of the eternal God, so that all the Gentiles might come to faith and obedience—to the only wise God be glory forever through Jesus Christ! Amen." (Rom. 16:25–27)

ON YOUR OWN:

Examine your heart for issues about which you disagree with other Christians—with an individual, a church, an organization. Focus on issues of Christian belief or practice. What feelings and attitudes do you have about those with whom you disagree? Ask God to bring to mind any individual or institution about whom you harbor feelings of judgment, scorn, or superiority. Ask him to show you whether the issues in question are essentials of the faith or disputable matters. Ask him to help you think about and deal with these people and issues in a Christlike way. Pray for yourself one or more of Paul's prayers above—for endurance and encouragement, for a spirit of unity, and so on.

NOTES

1. This section is based on *NIVAC: Romans*, 446–457.
2. Moo, 447.
3. Moo, 448.
4. Moo, 453.
5. Id.
6. Moo, 466.
7. This section is based on *NIVAC: Romans*, 458–476.
8. Moo, 468.
9. This section is based on *NIVAC: Romans*, 477–516.

LEADER'S NOTES

SESSION 1 LEADER'S NOTES

The primary goal of this session is to identify and begin to understand some of the themes that will recur throughout Romans. "What is the gospel?" is the central theme, but others are the relationship between Jews and Gentiles, the obedience of faith, righteousness, and the severity of sin that makes salvation necessary.

A second goal, especially if you are a new group, is to bond together as a group. Some questions throughout this study will ask participants to talk about their own lives, and to do that they will need a foundation of trust that others in the group respect what they have to say, want to know them, and won't talk about them outside the group. You might spend a couple of minutes setting those as ground rules.

Also, if you don't already know each other well, it can be helpful to start with a question that helps people say something nonthreatening about themselves. You might ask, "Given your background, what mental pictures or associations does the word "gospel" bring up for you?" As leader, you can set the tone by saying in just a sentence or two that it's a familiar—even over-familiar—word for you, because you grew up in a church where "preaching the gospel" was talked about a lot. Or, you didn't grow up in church, and for you "gospel" is a style of music.

1. God promised the gospel beforehand through his prophets in the Scriptures. The gospel is first and foremost about God's Son. It involves several key things about the Son's biography,

listed in 1:3–4. Later in Romans, Paul will come back to these biographical items (his connection with David, his resurrection, etc.) and explain why each is important. Further, the gospel involves grace, and the obedience that comes from faith. (You'll talk about faith and obedience in question 3.) It is "the power of God for the salvation of everyone who believes." (As a follow-up question, you might ask what it means to say the gospel is the power of God.) The gospel reveals a righteousness from God — you'll talk about what that means in questions 4 and 5.

2. If our main problem is alienation from ourselves and other people, then an effective spirituality might emphasize the insights and practices of psychotherapy, self-help and self-esteem, stress management, meditation to relieve anxiety, conflict resolution, and social justice. If our main problem is alienation from God, then we need a spirituality in which we and/or God do something to reconcile us to God and keep us reconciled. Romans 1:18–32 makes clear that Paul's gospel recognizes both our vertical and our horizontal problems. Yet Paul insists that our vertical problem must be addressed first, so Romans largely addresses vertical issues until chapter 12.

3. "Because [God] is holy, he cannot tolerate sin. Sin simply cannot exist in his presence. It is foreign to the essence of his being. God can no more exist in an atmosphere of sin than I can exist in a vacuum. Because he is just, he must punish sin. God can do anything, we sometimes think. But he cannot act in a way that violates his own nature .... Here, then, is the dilemma God himself faces. His love reaches out to us, sinful rebels that we are; but his holiness and justice prevent him from simply sweeping sin under the carpet. It must be punished."[1]

4. Real faith is active trust in a Person and commitment to his agenda in the world. There's much more to it than simply assenting to a body of information about Jesus.

5. There are many reasons. One is that the formative people among whom many of us have grown up don't model God's gracious acceptance. This will be a major struggle for some of your group members. Give them a few minutes to talk about that struggle, and try to keep others from giving them advice. Your group can be a place where people experience God's acceptance.

6. Some things that to Christians look plainly created and designed, to others look like the results of time and chance. It is worthwhile to play out the argument against Paul's claim and to look at its assumptions and conclusions. Paul says those assumptions come from futile thinking and darkened hearts (1:21). How can Paul say that some of the greatest minds of our age have futile thinking and darkened hearts? Is he just being unfair, or can you see why he thinks that?

7. Here are a few common idols: The individual self (elevated over any groups, including family, friends, church, school, society, the planet). Money. Sex. Youth. Political power. Freedom (personal freedom, free market, etc.). Notice that even things that are good in themselves (the individual, sex, freedom) can be turned into idols. Some of us idolize our families; others idolize work, or hobbies like photography or sports.

8. In our culture, promiscuity is rooted in the worship of the individual self. I decide what is right for me. I am essentially an animal with a sex drive that needs to be gratified. My sensual pleasure is of primary importance. The needs of the other person (for respect, for commitment, for care) are secondary. The needs of society are irrelevant.

9. It's easy to focus on the sins in Paul's list that don't appeal to us. But there is something in his list for all of us. We struggle with envy or deceit or gossip or sexual temptation. As an exercise, try committing yourself to eliminating deceit and malice from your life for the next week. No attempts to deceive anyone, no hostile thought or actions.

10. It might be worth reflecting on the ways gossip or deceit harm other people.

11. Give your group the freedom to say how they really feel about God's wrath. It's not a popular notion today. Question 12 gives them a chance to situate wrath within the larger context of God's gracious good news.

NOTE

1. Moo, 135–136.

SESSION 2 LEADER'S NOTES

The goals of this session are: (1) to help your group understand why Jews need Christ just as much as Gentiles do and, (2) to grapple with the idea of slavery or addiction to sin.

1. There is a vast difference between recognizing and even saying that someone else's behavior is wrong, and being smugly confident that we are better than they. Paul is criticizing judgment + hypocrisy and judgment + smugness.

2. God's kindness is supposed to motivate us to repentance — that is, to change our attitude and behavior. This is as true for Christians as for Jews. Scripture "teaches that a lack of concern about sin is incompatible with true faith."[1] A true Christian cares about getting free from sin and is willing to pay a price to do so.

3. Moo's commentary explains in detail why (e) is the best interpretation.[2] Paul is speaking hypothetically. In theory someone who lives up to God's pure holiness could win eternal life, but in practice we are all far too self-seeking to manage that. The other four alternatives all undercut Paul's overall argument in 1:18 – 3:20 that nobody, neither Jew nor Gentile, can stand before God with a clean conscience apart from Christ's sacrifice.

4. God might seem cruelly perfectionistic if we lose focus on two things: (1) he is by his own nature pure, scorching holiness. He is what he is. And (2) he has, at great cost to himself, provided Christ and the Holy Spirit to do for us and in us what we can't do on our own. You may want to let the scary picture of a holy and wrathful God stand for now until Romans 3 – 8 unfolds the rest of the the picture.

5. Those who believe in natural law argue that people of all cultures recognize qualities like generosity, concern for human life, sexual fidelity, and the keeping of promises as virtues. Individuals, social classes, or cultures devalue such virtues only when socially conditioned or psychologically deficient. The same can be said for seeing murder, adultery, incest, rape, and other acts as vices. Those who don't believe in natural law argue that all of these values and taboos are determined by societies. By that view, there's nothing inherently wrong with incest, sexual violence, human sacrifice, or anything else that a given society decides to permit.

6. This question covers the same ground as question 3 from another angle. It is here if you need repetition for emphasis, but you can move past it if you spent enough time on question 3.

7. "Some people may think that they are secure when they are not because they have never truly come to faith. They have 'walked up the aisle,' raised their hand at an invitation, or been baptized—but they have never truly submitted to Christ as Lord. Such people are not 'secure' in Christ."[3]

   Also, even genuine Christians can take their security for granted. The Bible says both that God will securely hang onto those who are his and that our obedience has some role to play in our destiny (see 8:12–13, for instance). That's a paradox. Our security in Christ should free us from anxiety, but it shouldn't make us so complacent that we imagine our actions don't matter.

8. For example, Paul speaks of the stubbornness and unrepentant hearts of his fellow Jews (2:5). Some feel Paul sounds sarcastic in 2:17–20, although Paul is perfectly serious in listing these very real advantages of being Jewish. Still, some people feel it's anti-Semitic just to say that Judaism doesn't provide salvation without Christ.

   There is a difference between "anti-Semitism" and "anti-Judaism."[4] The former is irrational hatred of the Jewish nation or people; the latter is opposition to the Jewish religion as ultimately a valid expression of the truth. Despite ingenious attempts to argue otherwise, the New Testament is certainly "anti-Jewish." That is, it contests the claim that the Old Testament is the final expression of God's truth and that people can find eternal salvation within the boundaries set down by Abraham, Moses, the prophets, and Torah.[4]

   As with all people, we need sympathetically to understand where Jews are coming from. Precisely because so many Jews resisted Jesus and the early church and because the first Christians had to define themselves over against the Jewish faith, we find a lot of polemic against Judaism in the New Testament. History, of course, is littered with the debris of Jewish-Christian debates and fights. With this behind us, it is easy to construct a caricature of the Jewish faith. Indeed, as recent work is revealing, Christian scholars in the past have often been guilty of misrepresenting the Jewish faith, portraying it as far more petty and legalistic than it really was.[5]

9. We should educate ourselves about Judaism in general and our particular friend in specific before we launch into the gospel. Two recommended books are *What Do Jews Believe?* by D. S. Ariel (New York: Schocken, 1995) and *An Introduction to Judaism* by N. de Lange (Cambridge: Cambridge University Press, 2000). It's also good to ask any individual what he or she believes, and spend a lot more time listening than talking. No one, Jewish or Gentile, should ever be just an evangelism project in our eyes.

10. "In an uncertain world, here is certainty; in a world without foundations, here is a rock-solid foundation."[6]

11. We are surrounded by people who "aren't that bad." Many do wonderful things. But without Christ, every one of them is enslaved to something—deceit, indifference to God, maybe something we can't guess. The fact that they behave better than we do is an indictment of us, not an excuse for them.

12. Far from condemning the sin addict, we should care profoundly for them. We know what it's like to be addicted to sin. We shouldn't be deceived if their lives seem fine, and we shouldn't avoid them if they're a mess.

NOTES

1. Moo, 80.
2. Moo, 80–81.
3. Moo, 109.
4. Moo, 100.
5. Moo, 100–101.
6. Moo, 108.

SESSION 3 LEADER'S NOTES

Romans 3:21 – 26 is the core of the letter, so it deserves revisiting. Your goal in this lesson is to understand as much as possible what Christ's death accomplished, why it was necessary. Ideally, you should walk away from this study able to explain the technical terms — atonement, righteousness, justification, grace — in plain English so you can talk about the gospel in ways an average person could connect with.

1. The Old Testament laid the groundwork for what God has now done in Christ. It's the same God, the same sin problem, the same need for righteousness. But this new thing God has done *provides* righteousness — right relationship with God — without the need to keep the Old Testament's laws.

2. Justice is essential to God's nature. It's uncompromising in that God can't tolerate sweeping injustice under a rug. There have to be consequences. It is in his very nature to loathe sin. An atonement sacrifice assumes that God has wrath that needs to be satisfied and turned away. It also assumes that sin is something defiling that we need to be cleansed from in order to approach a holy God. We might like God to be a little less like a scorching fire, but he is what he is. The wonder is that instead of expecting us to carry the consequences and achieve the cleansing, he did it himself, at great cost.

3. Nothing obligated the Father to offer the Son. Nothing obligated the Son to offer himself. Nothing we could do could make us deserve to have Christ pay the price for us.

4. This is a deep question. At a simplistic level, giving requires both a giver and a receiver. Faith is, at a minimum, truly receiving and truly saying "thank you." Also, the gift God offers is a right relationship. And like giving, relationship requires two involved parties. Faith is the most essential element of our side of the relationship.

5. On one hand, it is enough for us to be simply human and imperfect, because Christ carries the costs of our imperfections and mere humanness. In this life, we will never get beyond being imperfect humans. But we were made for more. There's a huge but subtle difference between perfectionism (which rejects limitations) and aspiring to the full glory we were

created for (which embraces limitations now in the hope of glory, by grace, hereafter).

6. Which best describes you before Christ: the depraved self-worshiper of 1:18 – 32? the hardhearted, pious hypocrite of 2:1 – 11? the venomous tongue of 3:11 – 18? Hard for some of us to imagine, but true nonetheless. And on top of that, unforgiven and destined for the full consequences of your choices. Because of Christ you're able to see the truth about yourself and God more clearly; you're forgiven for your faults; your relationship with God is restored; and you have the capacity to become like Christ. And that's just the beginning, as Romans 5 and following lay out.

7. From this reflection comes gratitude, motivation to love and serve your Rescuer, and renewed enthusiasm when life is difficult and your first experience of Christ was long ago.

8. Paul talks about boasting in 3:27 and again in 4:2. Not even Abraham had the right to boast, because even he owed his friendship with God to God's grace and his own humble response of faith, not to any of his heroic acts of obedience. One harm of boasting is that it stifles worship. "As long as we think, however subconsciously, that we have contributed something to our salvation, we will not put God on as high a plane as we should."[1] Also, boasting dooms us to an emotional roller coaster — of ego when we're doing well, and humiliation when we mess up.

9. You might be tempted to seek validation from your career, your children's intelligence or moral behavior, your church attendance, your volunteer work — any area where you're trying to live up to God's or other people's expectations in order to feel good about yourself.

10. God promises that he loves you no matter what you've done. He promises that you don't have to live up to his expectations in order to have a relationship with him. He promises that you have eternal life. He promises that your life is valuable and will be fruitful. You will encounter many more promises just in Romans.

11. Trusting God is an attitude, an orientation of the will you have because you believe it makes sense. Some people are naturally more emotional than others, but faith is something you have based on intuition or evidence that seems convincing. You can pray with faith that God is good and takes your

prayers into account, and it doesn't matter if you have feelings of hope or fear as you pray.

12. God's righteousness is a process. He takes action. He takes action to put us in right relationship with himself. It's about relationship. It starts with God's initiative, sacrificing his Son. Just how Christ's death atones for our sin is a deep matter, but it does. We need to respond with faith, but that right relationship is God's gift to us.

NOTE

1. Moo, 142.

SESSION 4 LEADER'S NOTES

The main goal of this session is to understand the benefits of justification by faith in Christ. However, the contrast between life "in Adam" and "in Christ" raises other issues, like original sin and the eternal destiny of unbelievers. You'll need to decide how much group time to devote to each issue.

1. Peace with God, access into grace, the hope of the glory of God, the experience of God's love poured into our hearts, joy even in suffering (also perseverance and character), salvation from God's wrath, reconciliation with God.

2. While we usually think of "salvation" as something we have now, Paul often uses the word for something we'll need later, on judgment day. For those of us who are aware of our imminent death or who have lost a loved one, what happens after death can be a burning issue. If death is out of sight and out of mind for us, eternity may feel like a "so what?" subject. Such denial can be a spiritual problem, yet there is some value in focusing on the here and now. In this life, peace with God should silence the inner voices that tell some of us, "God doesn't love you. Nothing you do is enough. You're a failure. You've messed up too badly."

3. For example, what we accomplish in ministry or work doesn't make us feel superior or inferior to someone else, because anything good we do comes because God graciously works through us.

4. As we saw in Romans 3:23, God's glory is his awesome presence and the eternal destiny of believers. Sharing in God's glorious presence and likeness isn't the number-one thing many of us long for. We may long for love from some person, respect, pain relief, achievement, significance, things that give us pleasure, or simply food and shelter. What we long for says a lot about who we are and determines the priorities of our time, energy, and money.

5. For example, suffering builds hope rather than despair when we're convinced in the midst of it that God loves us, can use our suffering for our own or others' good, and has a good long-range plan for us.

   Yes, [Paul] says in effect, I know Christians will continue to suffer. But life's difficulties do not contradict what I have been saying about the wonderful blessings of being a Christian; in fact, God actually uses them to bring us even greater blessing.

The key is the way we respond to the difficult trials that come our way. What we must do is to recognize that God uses them to build into our lives "perseverance" ([Greek,] *hypomone*; cf. 2:7; also "endurance," 15:4–5), which, in turn, leads to "character" ([Greek,] *dokime,* the quality that comes from having been "proved"; cf. 2 Cor. 2:9; 8:2; 9:13; 13:3; Phil. 2:22). Then we can truly "rejoice" in the midst of suffering, knowing that God is at work even in these evil things to bring us blessing. Paradoxically, Paul claims at the end of verse 4, suffering can actually lead to "hope." Just as resistance to a muscle strengthens it, so challenges to our hope can strengthen it.[1]

6. Christ's death for us when we didn't deserve it is the chief evidence of his love. Active love from fellow Christians can help make that truth concrete when we're going through something hard.

7. We don't earn any of the good things God does for us. It's all a gift, and the sensible response is deep gratitude.

8. We may be tempted to think that a God who is capable of wrath is also stingy or grudging in his gifts. We need to see him as abundantly generous. We don't live in scarcity, in "not enough." We live in abundance, overflowing grace, more than enough to compensate for our failures or life's difficulties.

9. Use your imagination. The news is full of images that depict death's reign. Picture yourself fully alive, whole, safe, glorious.

10. For example, business flourishes with the least possible amount of government regulation. But with too little regulation, the people who run businesses may hide problems with their products, or may pursue short-term financial gain over the long-term good of the environment. Law needs to take into account the fact that both governments and businesses are run by sinners who are inclined to put their self-interest ahead of others.

11. This is an emotional subject that you may have covered in session 1. See *NIVAC: Romans,* 192–193.

12. The benefits of faith in Christ should encourage us, but issues like original sin and the eternal destiny of unbelievers are bound to raise questions.

Some may also have questions about how, in their own lives, suffering can lead to hope.

Views on original sin fall into three categories (greatly simplified here):

a. *Imitation.* There is no "*real* connection between our sin and Adam's. What Adam did was to set a bad example for us that the rest of us have all followed. This view is generally considered to be suborthodox."[2] It denies Paul's clear teaching about a connection between our sin and Adam's, and it fails to explain the universality of sin. Why do *all* of Adam's children imitate his turning away from God?

b. *Infection.* " 'One trespass' contaminated human nature; this 'infection' has been passed down to all Adam's posterity. Everyone therefore sins, and as a result everyone is condemned."[3]

c. *Inclusion.* "Adam's sin is, at the same time, the sin of everyone else as well."[4]

NOTES

1. Moo, 171.
2. Moo, 189.
3. Moo, 190.
4. Id.

SESSION 5 LEADER'S NOTES

1. Paul sees baptism as part of the seamless set of events that mark our conversion. He doesn't seem interested in sorting out exactly what the ritual of water—distinct from our choices of repentance and faith—does for us. For him, all of these are a package that marks a crucial break from an old way of being (connected with sin) to a new one (connected with Christ). This break is so decisive that it amounts to a death and resurrection. Our relationship to sin is dramatically changed.

2. This issue gives you a chance to think about how your own context and experience affects the way you read the Bible. It's nearly impossible for modern Christians to talk about Paul's brief reference to baptism without reading into it their own experience—maybe their upbringing in a church where infant baptism was practiced but personal faith wasn't emphasized; or their upbringing in a church where infant baptism was unthinkable but they felt peer pressure to profess faith and be baptized at some age; or their moving experience of conversion and baptism as a young adult; and so on. If you tackle this question, invite the group to reflect on how their experience colors the degree to which they value baptism.

3. Our habits are so deeply ingrained that we still sin, even as Christians. Those habits are so strong that they seem to compel us. If we believe, deep down, that we're stuck with our sins, then we're off the hook from having to change. But if we accept Paul's view that sin no longer has the power to control us, we have to face our ingrained habits and ask, "Why am I still clinging to you?"

4. In Paul's mind, commitment to Christ brings so decisive a break in our relationship to sin that it's like a death. It's like changing sides in a war. Saying yes to Christ inherently means saying no to sin. Of course, we can still lie to ourselves about some particular sin, some habit that feeds a perceived need that we hate to let go of, but truly encountering Christ fundamentally changes our relationship to sin.

5. The essential similarity is that we really do live in a different country—the country of Christ rather than sin—but our minds and bodies are so habituated to the country of sin that we often forget who and where we are. If the soldier metaphor doesn't work for some group members, here's another:

We're like children who have moved from an abusive home to a loving home. We have a new parent with new and loving rules, but it takes time and effort to stop reacting to situations as if we were still in the abusive home.

6. One of the main things we need to do is to keep reminding ourselves of who we are: reconciled to God, alive to God, loved by God, filled with the Holy Spirit; and dead to sin, no longer compelled to live the way we did. We need to keep our new identity clear and conscious in our thinking throughout the day. Simple practices can help with this, such as reading a portion of Scripture in the morning and reflecting on it throughout the day; or posting a sentence or two of Scripture about our identity on the car dashboard so we're reminded of it; or keeping a picture of Christ on the cross on our desk to remind us of our own death to sin. There's more to uprooting deeply ingrained habits than these practices, but they can help to refocus our thinking.

7. Consider a man who isn't by nature physically affectionate with his children. He might decide to offer his hands to God for the purpose of expressing love to them. He might begin by deciding to warmly lay a hand on each child's shoulder once a day. Perhaps a gentle squeeze of the shoulder. If you're a natural hugger, this might sound like a small thing, but for some people it's a major step.

8. Paul says sin enslaves even the nicest non-Christian. Some of us find it hard to believe this about our considerate coworker or generous friend. Others of us are intensely aware of the flaws in everyone. Paul isn't saying that non-Christians generally do worse things than Christians do (sadly, this is too often not the case), but that a life not oriented toward God is inevitably oriented toward self. What would Paul say about the Buddhist who tirelessly gives himself to help poor people or refugees? Isn't that person oriented toward giving to others rather than self? Only God knows the heart, and the point here definitely isn't to make group members feel smugly superior to non-Christians. Perhaps God wants us to grow more like the compassionate Buddhist in some ways while recognizing that that person still has a desperate need for God that we might be blind to.

9. Sins of the mouth: gossip, complaining, criticism that doesn't build others up. Sins of the hands: violence, withholding affection, inward rage

expressed in a clenched fist. Accumulating possessions can reflect a belief that being physical creatures means spending money to adorn our bodies, improve our bodies, feel the engine and smell the leather of a new car, feed our eyes with expensive things, and so on. To be human is to have a body, and that means we're designed to respond to beautiful sights, sounds, and smells, to enjoy physical comforts and pleasure. Christian faith doesn't mean suppressing that physicality, but rather respecting it and making choices about how to channel it.

10. Some channels are the Bible, prayer, worship with others, discussions about faith, music, silence, service, and so on. We do such things not to earn favor with God but to give him opportunities to fill us with grace to be who we're meant to be. If you're doing such things regularly and aren't aware of experiencing grace through them, it's worthwhile to talk through with the group why that might be the case.

11. If we fill our lives with noise and busyness, we shut off the channels through which God wants to give us grace to live fruitfully. "Letting go" is helpful if it means shutting off the noise and spending regular time in stillness before God, but not if it means passively rushing through modern life and expecting God to make our lives magically work out.

12. You could talk about *any* sin; gossip is simply a concrete example that people aren't embarrassed to talk about. God's job is to convict the gossip of her (it could equally be his) sin, to forgive her, to provide grace for genuine repentance, to give the Holy Spirit to empower change. The gossip's job is to give mental attention to examining her life on a regular basis so she can hear God convict her, to confess her sin to him, to take time to reflect on what drives her to talk about others, perhaps to talk to a friend about this habit, to deliberately offer her tongue to God for use in building others up, to pray for grace to notice when she's gossiping, to listen to herself when she's with the people she often gossips to, to keep persistently confessing when she realizes she's done it again, to pray for grace to change, perhaps to meditate on Scriptures about the love of neighbor or the use of the tongue, to look for positive things to say about others, and so on. This isn't a formula, but rather a list of examples. As we'll see in Romans 8, she may need to decide to feed her mind a diet of stories, ideas, and images that foster kindness and generosity, or stop feeding her

mind a diet of television shows in which people routinely gossip about each other.

Reminding herself about the new regime will help her feel how absurd and wrong gossip is for a person who lives in Christ. How it doesn't fit with her true identity. How she doesn't need it to feel like a valuable person—she doesn't need to tear others down in order to build herself up.

SESSION 6 LEADER'S NOTES

1. The Jewish Christians had grown up keeping the law. They were probably emotionally attached to it as the way a godly person lives. They needed to get clear in their minds that while it was still fine for them to live that way, they shouldn't look down on—or question the salvation of—Gentile Christians who chose not to live that way. It was also important for both groups to be protected from the arrogance of believing there was something they could do to obligate God. Finally, law-keeping was a potential barrier to evangelism among Gentiles. Many Gentiles were drawn to the Jewish God but unwilling to take on the customs (especially circumcision) of Jewish culture.

2. This is similar to what Paul said in Romans 6 about being slaves of righteousness. Christian freedom is freedom to do what God made us to do in the world, not freedom to indulge ourselves. Again, Paul assumes that no real Christian is interested in self-indulgence; any real Christian longs to bear fruit for God.

3. Serving in the new way of the Spirit involves serving by the power of the Spirit, and serving according to the New Testament model of life. "Christian obedience is the reflection of the Spirit's work in transforming our minds and hearts. But commandments are needed to guide that transforming work. God has therefore given us in the New Testament specific commands to direct our conduct and to show us when we are straying from his moral will."[1] Christians aren't just dead to the civil and ceremonial laws of the Old Testament; we're dead to the old covenant. We are, however, expected to obey those commands given in the New Testament. That includes at least nine of the Ten Commandments (Sabbath-keeping isn't commanded in the New Testament, and Christians debate its place in our lives).

4. It's important to underscore that obeying New Testament commands doesn't earn salvation or God's love. It is simply the "bearing fruit for God" and living as "slaves of righteousness" that Paul speaks of elsewhere. We lack the willpower to do this in our strength without the Spirit's power, but nothing in Paul's writings indicates that bearing fruit is automatic or effortless for us.

5. He says, "Once I was alive apart from the law" (7:9). This was never true of him as an individual—he was born under the law and dead in sin. He's speaking of Israel as a whole. But he does say things that are true of him as an individual as well as true of his people: perhaps he wouldn't have been aware that coveting was a sin except through the law (7:7).

6. This may be hard for us because our culture emphasizes individualism.

7. Even the moral code of a Christian society can have this effect on young people who grow up experiencing the commands but not the love of Christ. For them, Christ's commands (and the extra rules of their subculture) may just bring sinful desires to the surface and make them long to break out.

8. The law of Moses didn't come with power from the Holy Spirit to obey it adequately. Those who are in Adam have something driving them that is so strong that Paul can call it a "law of sin" (7:23). They are slaves of sin (7:14), and the law of Moses has no power to free them.

9. As leader, you might benefit your group by being honest if you see yourself in this text. Others may be ashamed to admit it, but they may need to.

10. Those who think this passage is about Paul as a mature Christian "think this text provides warrant for thinking that the Christian life will be marked by continuing struggle with sin. Let me make clear that while I [Moo] do not agree with their interpretation of Romans 7, I certainly agree with the larger point. Paul makes abundantly clear elsewhere (e.g., Rom. 6:11–13; Gal. 5:17; Eph. 6:10–17) that believers have a never-ending fight on their hands to put into practice the victory over sin we experience in Christ. My problem with taking Romans 7 as a description of this struggle ... is that Paul does not just describe a struggle here (e.g., 7:15–20); he describes a struggle that ends in frustration and defeat (7:21–25).

    "This is not true to Paul's understanding of the Christian life. Our 'death to sin' (ch. 6), the indwelling power of the Holy Spirit (ch. 8), and the renewal of our minds (12:1–2) will inevitably mean that we sin less and less. Yes, we will never become sinless, but we will certainly *sin less*. Paul does not seem to reflect this in Romans 7, however, nor do the negative tones of verses 21–25 fit the eventual victory that is ours in Christ."[2]

    Intense struggle against sin is part of a "normal" Christian life, but relentless defeat in the struggle isn't. Perhaps many of us see ourselves in this passage because we've never been taught how to cooperate with the

Holy Spirit in overcoming sin, or because we've never committed ourselves to the time and attention it involves, or because we're trying to do it on our own when a community of friends is one of the channels of grace God needs us to take advantage of.

11. They need understanding, a listening ear, encouragement without judgment. It can be helpful to have someone (or a few) we can go to, perhaps monthly (or in some cases weekly or daily for a while), to say, "Here's how I'm doing." This isn't someone who checks up on us and tells us what to do, but someone who is willing to pray with and for us.

12. One thing Christians can do is to build enough of a friendship with such people that they can see how we deal with our weaknesses through confession, the desire to change, and gratitude for forgiveness.

NOTES

1. Moo, 222.
2. Moo, 245–246.

SESSION 7 LEADER'S NOTES

1. He says "if anyone does not have the Spirit of Christ, he does not belong to Christ" (8:9). "We may not always reflect [the control of the Spirit] (see 8:12 – 13), but it is a fundamental fact of our Christian existence and the basis for a life of confidence and obedience to the Lord."[1]

   But "controlled by" doesn't mean controlled like a robot. We are citizens and subjects of the Spirit's domain, not the flesh's — that is our identity. But we still have the option to choose whether we'll live in accord with that identity or slip back into old habits. We can live like the adopted and loved children we are, or like orphans doing whatever we can to survive.

2. It doesn't happen automatically because this is the way God made us. Habits are deeply ingrained, automatic responses. Our brains and bodies are designed to learn (or unlearn) habits over time. God wants spiritual growth to be a partnership that requires chosen intimacy between us and him. He doesn't want it to happen by magic any more than a good parent wants to hand all of life to her children on a platter, protecting them from any effort.

3. It feels good in the short run. The flesh aims to maximize pleasure and minimize pain for itself.

5. We may never have learned how to engage with God creatively and passionately. Our models may be genuinely dull. On the other hand, engaging our minds with anything deeper than entertainment takes effort. It takes time. And while a life of prayer yields periods of euphoria, God doesn't give us constant ecstasy lest we pursue good feelings rather than him. And the Scriptures shine light on parts of our hearts that we might more comfortably ignore.

6. The Holy Spirit testifies that we are God's children and heirs, that glory lies ahead, and that this life of groaning is temporary. And God promises that no matter what happens, he is working for our ultimate good. Things can be extremely painful in the short and medium term, but nothing can ultimately harm us.

7. Faith maintains confidence that a baby (or glory) lies at the end of the struggle. It doesn't require us to put on a happy face in the midst of anguish.

8. "Essentially, [8:28] promises that nothing will touch our lives that is not under the control and direction of our loving heavenly Father. Everything we do and say, everything people do to us or say about us, every experience we will ever have—all are sovereignly used by God for our good. We will not always understand how the things we experience work to good, and we certainly will not always enjoy them. But we do know that nothing comes into our lives that God does not allow and use for his own beneficent purposes."[2]

9. People might feel a whole range of feelings from relief to frustration to joy to yearning. But just as the ultimate promise of a baby makes a woman bear pregnancy and labor with courage rather than despair, so our hope of glory should enable us to live graciously and bravely even when this life is frustrating.

10. Courage, joy, zeal.

11. Put in the time and effort involved in putting to death the habits of the flesh and thus living according to the Spirit.

12. "Security without responsibility breeds passivity, but responsibility without security leads to anxiety.

"I [Moo] have counseled both types of Christians. During an interim pastorate, I got to know an elder in the church. He proclaimed himself a strong Calvinist and delighted to discuss Reformed theology. I eventually discovered that he was having sex outside his marriage. But he was not worried about it; he was eternally secure in Christ. I also remember counseling a young woman who was extremely performance oriented. She brought this attitude into her Christianity and was eternally in despair because she had not lived up to the Lord's expectations of her. She could not grasp her security in Christ—that Christ had taken her sins so that her performance was no longer the basis for her acceptance....

"I like the careful balance Paul achieves in verse 13: 'By the *Spirit you* put to death the misdeeds of the body' (italics added). Paul puts the responsibility squarely on our shoulders: *You* need to put sin to death. But at the same time, he makes it clear that we can only do it *through the Spirit*."[3]

NOTES

1. Moo, 251.
2. Moo, 278.
3. Moo, 258–259.

SESSION 8 LEADER'S NOTES

1. He feels such anguish because they are his family. Don't go off on a long digression about your loved ones, but it's helpful to bring those people to mind as you begin this conversation.
2. Some might see this God as unfair, but in fact this God is completely in control and not at all beholden to anybody.
3. Some might feel more comfortable with a God we could predict and control, who owed us something. But the more we're aware of how utterly not in control of our worlds we are, the happier we'll be that God has things under control, and the more grateful we will be for grace.[1]
4. God hardened Pharaoh's heart, so that Pharaoh would not free the Israelite slaves. Thus God could display his power by afflicting Egypt with plagues, so that all the neighboring nations would hear about his great might.
5. Paul thinks the Creator has a right to make a person with whatever personality and for whatever purposes he wants.
6. It's very important for group members to be able to voice their praise or mistrust. Christians disagree sharply on the relationship between God's sovereignty and human freedom taught in this passage, and they have strongly different emotional reactions. Nothing is gained by mistrusting God and keeping those feelings to oneself. A group should be a safe place to express even negative feelings about God. Voicing feelings can be an important step on the way to reconciling them and trusting God more fully.
7. Here Paul gives the other side of the coin, the side of human responsibility. Having attributed the Jews' situation to election, he now says they are responsible for their situation because they choose to pursue righteousness through the law.
8. Both grace and faith are essential to salvation. Paul emphasizes both. Grace, or God's sovereignty, is primary, but faith is still necessary.
9. We should continue to read, study, and meditate on the Old Testament, because it lays the foundation for our understanding of God, Christ, faith, and many other things. We are no longer obligated to obey its commands, except those that are repeated or implied in the New Testament, but the law can teach us a great deal about what God values.

10. Paul's heart might ache as he pleads with Aaron to see that Christ is the fulfillment and goal of the law he loves.

11. Paul might think God has hardened Richard's heart or that Richard has hardened his own heart. Paul would be confident that God chooses whom he wishes, but that wouldn't for a moment make Paul passive in relating to Richard. He would treat Richard with every kindness and respect, and would both live and explain his faith in terms Richard might be able to digest. He would likely encourage Richard's sister to do the same, not with anxiety but with confidence in God's goodness. And he wouldn't quit praying.

12. "Caving in to the flood of postmodern malaise and afraid of seeming intolerant, many churches have lost missionary zeal. Reasons vary, of course. But some teach that other religions are also ways to God, so why bother sending missionaries if people can be saved within their own religion? Others teach that God reveals himself to all people in various ways, so that an oral or written presentation of the gospel is unnecessary.

   "But the text before us shows such viewpoints as the false teachings or easy generalizations they really are. Paul links salvation to belief, which he in turn ties to hearing the message about Christ. . . .

   "I [Moo] do not want to minimize the problems inherent in a theology that ties salvation to response to God's Word. I, too, struggle with the question of fairness, wondering about those many people who never had a chance to respond to the Word of God. And I do not want to dogmatize beyond the text about the ways in which God may bring his message to people.

   "But I do think Romans 10:14–21, in the context of Paul's life and theology, teaches that response to God's Word is the only way to salvation and that sending out people to proclaim that Word is God's chosen way to bring that Word 'to the ends of the earth.' "[2]

NOTES

1. For details on why we think Paul is talking about individuals, see *NIVAC: Romans*, 304–308.
2. Moo, 351–352.

SESSION 9 LEADER'S NOTES

1. On the idea of a remnant, see 9:6–8. On the idea that they are the elect (that is, chosen by God), see 9:11–12, 16. On Jews who are hardened, see 9:16–18, 30–32 and 10:21.

2. The benefits can include a commitment to holiness, resisting the temptation to water down the faith with the values, attitudes, and preoccupations of the surrounding culture. The risks include spiritual pride (feeling superior to other Christians), isolating oneself from the balancing influence that Christians from other points of view (and different blind spots) can offer, refusing to join together with other Christians to pursue God's work in the world, and ineffectiveness in communicating the gospel to unbelievers.

3. Many Jews thought that belonging to their ethnic group and participating in its rites (circumcision, etc.) satisfied God, so a personal allegiance to Jesus Christ wasn't necessary. Even Christians who grow up in communities that theoretically teach the need for a personal relationship with Christ can mistakenly think their habit of church participation (perhaps including an altar call) qualifies as a saving relationship with Christ.

4. The Jews' rejection of Christ inadvertently made possible the gospel's spread through Gentile cultures. If the early church had remained largely Jewish culturally, it would have been hard for the church to see that the gospel doesn't belong to any one ethnic culture but stands above all of them.

5. If Gentile believers were the majority in Rome, it might have been easy for them to look down on Jews, most of whose kinsmen had rejected Christ. This has been a serious problem in Christian societies for centuries. But anti-Semitism in any form is both sinful and foolish, first because the Jews continue to have a special place in God's plan, and second because Gentiles don't deserve salvation any more than Jews do. Many Gentile Christians throughout history have blamed the Jews for killing Christ, but Paul sees Gentiles as equally guilty before God.

6. Most of us need to invest a great deal more energy into learning what the Old Testament can teach us about the gospel, our Jewish Messiah, and God's centuries-long plan for the world. We can also learn from the ways

Jewish scholars have reflected on their Scriptures. Passover can teach us about the meaning of Easter, Yom Kippur (the Day of Atonement) can teach us about Christ's sacrifice of atonement, and so on. Listening to ordinary Jews talking about their faith can be extremely enlightening.

7. "The tension ... is part of the larger interplay of God's sovereignty and human responsibility that is so difficult to untangle in Scripture.... [W]e have essentially three options. (1) We can give full credit to both perspectives without resolving the tension. (2) We can acknowledge that God has limited his sovereignty to allow for genuine human decisions (essentially, the Arminian view). (3) We can maintain God's absolute sovereignty while limiting the freedom of human actions (essentially the Calvinist view).

"... If we are to preserve the tension while giving Paul credit as a consistent and systematic thinker, we can only resort, I [Moo] think, to the idea of mystery. Paul teaches both that salvation for the believer is assured and that a believer can lose his or her salvation, and we must leave the reconciliation of the two in the hands of God.

"Yet this approach also has its problems, for it comes close to believing an out-and-out contradiction. We surely must acknowledge that God's thoughts are far beyond ours and that many mysteries will remain in our understanding of the faith. But there is a difference between believing two things we cannot reconcile and believing two things that are contradictory.

"... Whatever we finally make of the theology of this warning [in 11:19–22], we must come to grips with the seriousness of Paul's warning here. Whether Calvinist or Arminian, we all recognize that our response to God's grace is necessary if we are to be saved. The arrogance and complacency of the Gentile Christians in Rome is all too easy an attitude to fall into—especially for those of us who are Calvinists![1]

8. This is a difficult passage. It may be helpful to look at a complete analysis, with other options in *NIVAC: Romans*, 377–380.

9. Paul leaves no room for anti-Semitism. We should continue to pray for Jews and to care about giving them an accurate view of Christ, because Paul foresees no salvation for anyone, including Jews, apart from Christ.

10. This could become a heated discussion, so you may need to emphasize ground rules of respect for different points of view.

11. Again, there may be raw feelings in the group on this subject. Some American Christians are unaware that there are significant numbers of Arab Christians (not all Arabs are Muslim), or may not think so-called Arab Christians are truly saved.

12. The big themes include God's sovereignty and human responsibility; God's heart for the Jews; and the need for humility and gratitude about your own salvation.

NOTE

1. Moo, 373–375.

SESSION 10 LEADER'S NOTES

1. These include being forgiven, having a relationship with God that is at peace, being so loved by God that nothing can come between you and him, being freed from slavery to sin, being God's adopted child and heir of glory, having the Holy Spirit who enables you to obey God and prays through you in your weakness, and so on.

2. You could start with your tongue: spend a week looking for opportunities to speak kind and truthful words. Or start with your driving (a very physical task), looking for chances to be courteous and patient. The point here isn't perfect performance, but noticing and seeking grace to act in love — or grace for forgiveness when you don't.

3. Fleeting upbeat emotions quickly fade; we've forgotten them by the time the opportunity arrives to offer ourselves in daily life. But worship rooted in who God is can shift the way we think all day and can instill more fruitful emotions, such as courage and compassion.

4. Some examples: "My time is more valuable than other people's." "Nobody else is allowed to make mistakes." "The other drivers on the road are not people with whom I am in relationship." "The other drivers on the road are blocking my goals."

5. There are no magic formulas, but here are some ideas. At the beginning of his day, he could read and reflect on a story of Jesus interacting with people. In Luke 8:40–56, for example, notice how Jesus responds when interrupted in the middle of an urgent agenda. The aggressive driver could try playing calm music or an upbeat recorded book while driving, and avoid aggressive music or angry talk radio shows.

   Renewing the mind is a process.

   "The fact that Paul calls on believers to engage in this renewing of the mind shows that it does not automatically happen to us when we believe. God's Spirit comes to reside in us, and he provides a whole new orientation to our thinking. But our thinking itself is not instantaneously changed. The ruts of the old life are not always easy to get out of....

   "The key question then becomes: What are we feeding into our minds? Most Christians have little choice but to spend forty or fifty hours of every week in 'the world,' making a living. It is hoped that most Christians also seek to spend time with unbelievers as a means of ministry and evangelism. But if we spend all our discretionary time watching network television, reading secular books, and listening to secular music, it will be a wonder if our minds are not fundamentally secular. Our job is to cooperate with God's Spirit by seeking to feed into our minds information that will reprogram our thinking in line with the values of the kingdom....

"God is at work in us, changing from within the very way that we think. This is a far better alternative than any law, for no law can conceivably cover all the issues we face in life. No matter how detailed, 'law' will always fail to cover some situations. We need to face squarely this limitation and its consequences."[1]

6. For example, churches can train members in how the mind influences emotions and behavior, and how the mind can be renewed. Preachers can address foundational biblical ideas that underlie ethical decision making: What does it mean to love one's neighbor? To love one's enemy? How does a Christian relate to the government? What does it mean to say that every human life is sacred, and what are the implications not just for the unborn, but from conception to the grave?

7. An inflated view of oneself is perhaps the greatest barrier to growth. It hinders us from seeing our blind spots. It encourages us to minimize our own shortcomings and maximize other people's shortcomings. It hinders us from valuing other people's perspectives and gifts. It makes us rigid and unforgiving.

8. We're designed to be interdependent. We can't do the work of God on our own, because we lack some vital gifts. Thus, we need others to serve God. We also need others to help us see and overcome our faults. We need them to help us understand Scripture. Also, others need us—our gifts and insights.

9. For instance, genuine love includes practical actions such as providing food or housing for those in need (Rom. 12:13), as well as attitudes such as devotion and honor (12:10).

10. "[Both Paul and Jesus] seem clearly to prohibit ... vengeance, that is, taking revenge by exacting justice from those who have done wrong to us.... [W]hat is clear is that believers are to cultivate an attitude of love that puts the focus on the good of the other person and not on the defense of our

own rights, dignity, or even, perhaps, our very lives. Lived out consistently, the Christian community can become a genuine counterculture that serves as a witness to a world increasingly caught up in the spiral of violence.

"Americans demand the right to carry guns and use them because other people are. Poverty-stricken nations spend billions of dollars on weapons so that they can keep up with their neighbors. Our children are taught to defend themselves, to 'fight for their rights,' and so on. Jesus suggests a better way. While it would be utopian for us to think we can transform society by our attitudes, what the church is ultimately called to do is to be a witness."[2]

11. Christians are in the world not for our own sake, but for the sake of the world. If we believe that our ultimate security is taken care of (Rom. 8:28), then caring for others' good and being a witness to the world can become a priority.

NOTES

1. Moo, 398–399.
2. Moo, 419.

SESSION 11 LEADER'S NOTES

1. We submit to governmental authorities because God has delegated power to them (Rom. 13:1–2) and because they serve the necessary task of punishing wrongdoers (13:3–4). We submit because our consciences tell us it's the right thing to do, and also for the practical reason that if we don't we'll be punished (13:5).

2. Christians in the American South in the 1950s disobeyed racial segregation laws in order to push for their repeal. This is called civil disobedience, and it has also been used against abortion laws and other laws that Christians have considered immoral.

3. Speed limits and tax laws tempt many Christians to disobedience.

4. Sometimes being nice isn't the same as being loving. Sometimes we need to confront someone about sin in order to do good to them or to those they are harming. But this needs to be done in a way that truly has the other's good at heart, not our own desire to vent anger and demonstrate our righteousness. Similarly, feelings of romantic affection aren't the best guide to what is okay sexually. If we truly love someone, we'll ask, "Will this sexual act harm him or her in the short or long term?" For example, there's evidence that a string of heavy petting relationships in one's teens and twenties causes real emotional harm to some people. Some find it hard to bond with a spouse after bonding and breaking up with a series of people. Married women in their thirties report loss of interest in sex that is tied to sexual experiences before marriage. What would happen if unmarried Christians were taught to ask, "Is this sexual act potentially harmful to my partner after we break up?" rather than "Is this sexual act technically okay because it's not 'going all the way'?"

5. This isn't an easy situation. But the potential harm done by the lie illustrates why the New Testament commands us not to lie. If this person tells the truth, it will be painful and cause some level of rupture in a relationship between two people. If this person lies, the relationships among three people are damaged. Can any of them trust each other if lies are necessary to keep the peace among them?

6. Legalism is obeying God's commands in order to deserve his approval, or to show others that we deserve God's approval. It's also legalistic to expand

on God's commands with cultural rules and treat them as equivalent. For instance, God tells us to behave decently (13:13). It used to be considered indecent for a woman to display her ankles in public. Today Christians are more likely to debate the decency of belly buttons. Treating the biblical command as something we're expected to figure out how to obey in our context isn't legalism. However, sometimes we get so caught up making rules to simplify decisions (belly buttons yes/no) that we fail to train ourselves and our children to think broadly about what God is asking of us: "What effect does my clothing have on people around me? What effect does the form of comedy in this movie have on me and my friends? How do I weigh freedom against harm in this situation?"

7. There isn't a formula, but some elements include taking daily time to reflect on the Bible's teachings about love and the ways Jesus and other biblical people treated others; selecting entertainment that helps us think constructively about how people treat each other, rather than entertainment that fosters carelessness about others; talking with other Christians about how to love; praying for the grace to love others better; and so on.

8. Thinking about Christ's return reminds us of who we are: people of the light. It also reminds us that we will have to give an account of our actions (2 Cor. 5:10). It also helps us think about the long term, so we can set aside short-term gratification.

9. There's no amount of short-term gratification that can compensate for eternity. A month seems incredibly long to a five-year-old, and seventy years seems long to us. But it isn't.

10. Sexual desires often come to mind first, but our flesh is equally prone to excessive craving for money, control, being number one in a group, possessions, payback against those who hurt us or block our goals, food, drink, the adrenalin rush of various forms of entertainment—the list could go on.

11. As noted earlier, legalistic rules often fail to help us live in ways that please God because we set them either too narrowly or too broadly. For instance, narrow sexual rules make many unmarried Christians think that only one act counts as sexual immorality, and everything else is fair game. Such a rule ignores how sexual behavior really affects people. It ignores the possibility of harming oneself or the other person. Narrow rules are often reactions against overly broad rules of generations past. More useful than

narrow or broad rules of this kind are questions like, "How does a person of the daylight live? What entertainment feeds a mind to live in light versus darkness? What is decent behavior? Am I doing this out of Christian freedom, or am I seeking to gratify my flesh/sinful nature?"

SESSION 12 LEADER'S NOTES

1. We don't look down on another because God has accepted her. She is God's servant and answerable to him, not us. We need to trust that she's doing this practice "to the Lord" (14:6) — out of love for him — and if she isn't, she's answerable to him for that when she stands before the judgment seat.

2. Just making this list together may raise sparks in the room if some feel that a practice is okay, while others feel it falls under the category of indecent (13:13) or doctrinally wrong. (Belly buttons? Baptism without full immersion? Alcohol?) See if you can practice Paul's teaching against dissension while putting your issues on the table.

3. You'll know how much trust you've built in the group by the level of honesty here. As leader, you might do your group a service by being honest here yourself.

4. Obviously, the Bible is our standard here. But on issues where the Bible's teaching isn't clear-cut, each community needs to make decisions prayerfully and with an eye to the wisdom Christians today and in generations past can offer.

   Regarding the core teachings of the gospel, the Nicene Creed (formulated in the fourth and fifth centuries AD as a result of extensive study and debate of Scripture) is the early church's effort to form a basis of agreement. "Most churches and denominations will want to express their own distinctive approach to the faith by adding certain doctrines to the list. But we should be careful about insisting that such additions are essential to the faith and therefore a basis for fellowship with other believers."[1]

5. It's not easy to just get over an element of conscience. Paul implies that he hopes that over time the weak will think about their stance in light of Scripture and gradually revise their views. But ignoring the voice of our conscience in one area can backfire by making us insensitive or confused about right and wrong in other areas.

6. Righteousness (behavior that pleases God), peace in the Christian community, and the joy that results from these are priorities (14:18). So is building others up (14:19). Paul doesn't say so here, but elsewhere he shows that he uses his Christian freedom to spread the gospel in cultures where customs

differ (1 Cor. 9:19–23). He does things that conservative Jewish Christians aren't comfortable with in order to show Gentiles that the gospel isn't captive to one culture's rules. But he exercises that freedom for the sake of others (the Gentiles), not to indulge himself.

7. Dave should review Paul's instructions to the strong. Allen should review what Paul says to the weak. Then they can discuss this situation with an eye toward righteousness, peace, and joy, not toward winning or proving themselves superior.

8. Allen needs to remind himself that Dave is accountable to God, not him. Dave needs to remind himself that Christ died for Allen. In this way, they can forgive and love each other, free of resentment despite this disagreement. They might feel some sadness about the disagreement, but not anger, resentment, or contempt.

9. For example, Luke 4:1–6:11 shows Jesus maintaining his focus on pleasing God amid the swirling expectations of others and the temptations to satisfy himself. He extends himself to heal people, but he doesn't mind angering the people of Nazareth or Capernaum when their expectations are unreasonable. He makes no effort to please the Pharisees and teachers of the law when he thinks they're wrong about what God commands. Like Paul, he uses his freedom for the sake of sinners and those in need. Pleasing himself doesn't seem to be a strong motivation. Yet as King of God's kingdom, Jesus claims authority to revise one of God's commands, the Sabbath.

10. First, it's important to think through whether the issue is fundamental to the gospel or a disputable matter. If the latter, then all the principles laid out in this section of Romans will be helpful: righteousness, peace, joy, building others up, avoiding contempt for others, letting God judge them, and so on.

11. If you're tight on time, you can skip this question and just use these passages for worship (see "Responding to God's Word").

12. It will be valuable to let each person say something about what they got out of this study. It's good to celebrate where you've come together and thank each other for what you've received.

NOTE

1. Moo, 466.

The NIV Application Commentary

Romans

Douglas J. Moo

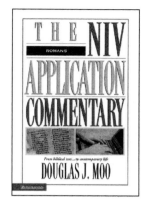

Most Bible commentaries take us on a one-way trip from our world to the world of the Bible. But they leave us there, assuming that we can somehow make the return journey on our own. In other words, they focus on the original meaning of the passage but don't discuss its contemporary application. The information they offer is valuable—but the job is only half done!

The NIV Application Commentary helps us with both halves of the interpretive task. This new and unique series shows readers how to bring an ancient message into a modern context. It explains not only what the Bible meant but also how it can speak powerfully today.

Our culture does not encourage thoughtful reflection on truth. Yet living the gospel in a postmodern culture demands that Christians understand and internalize the truth about God and his plan for the world. Paul's letter to the Romans remains one of the most important expressions of Christian truth ever written. Its message forces us to evaluate who we are, who God is, and what our place in this world ought to be. Going beyond the usual commentary, this volume brings the meaning of Paul's great letter into the twenty-first century. Douglas Moo comments on the text and then explores issues in Paul's culture and in ours that help us understand the ultimate meaning of each paragraph. A final section suggests ways in which the eternal theology of Romans can be understood and lived out in our modern culture.

Hardcover, Printed: 978-0-310-49400-3

Pick up a copy today at your favorite bookstore!

Share Your Thoughts

With the Author: Your comments will be forwarded to the author when you send them to *zauthor@zondervan.com*.

With Zondervan: Submit your review of this book by writing to *zreview@zondervan.com*.

Free Online Resources at
www.zondervan.com/hello

 Zondervan AuthorTracker: Be notified whenever your favorite authors publish new books, go on tour, or post an update about what's happening in their lives.

 Daily Bible Verses and Devotions: Enrich your life with daily Bible verses or devotions that help you start every morning focused on God.

 Free Email Publications: Sign up for newsletters on fiction, Christian living, church ministry, parenting, and more.

 Zondervan Bible Search: Find and compare Bible passages in a variety of translations at www.zondervanbiblesearch.com.

 Other Benefits: Register yourself to receive online benefits like coupons and special offers, or to participate in research.